Quiet Resolution

Quiet Resolution

Quebec's Challenge to Canada

GEORGES MATHEWS

Summerhill Press, ***Toronto***

Published by Summerhill Press Ltd.
52 Shaftesbury Avenue, Toronto, Ontario M4T 1A2

Distributed by University of Toronto Press
5201 Dufferin Street, Downsview, Ontario M3H 5T8

Cover design by Linda Gustafson

Printed and bound in Canada

Canadian Cataloguing in Publication Data

Mathews, Georges, 1946-
Quiet resolution

Translation of: L'Accord: comment Robert Bourassa fera l'indépendance.
Includes bibliographical references.
ISBN 0-929091-35-3

1. Quebec (Province) - Politics and government - 1960- . 2. Nationalism - Quebec (Province). 3. Federal government - Canada. 4. Federal-provincial relations - Canada. 5. Canada. Constitution Act, 1982. 6. Canada - Constitutional laws - Amendments.

JL246.S8M3813 1990 971.4'04 C90-095283-0

To Christine
in memory of
an incandescent season

While writing this book I benefited from the services of the Institut national de la recherche scientifique (section Urbanisation), and I wish to thank Roxane Petit for her speed and competence in handling the word processing.

Special thanks are due to Christine Saillart, who read and corrected the French manuscript in a strict and balanced spirit.

Translated by Dominique Clift

Contents

Foreword to the English Edition

This essay was written in the first months of 1990 and published in Quebec at the end of April, under the title *L'Accord — Comment Robert Bourassa fera l'indépendance* (The Accord — How Robert Bourassa Will Lead Quebec to Independence). I was convinced that the failure of the Meech Lake Accord, inevitable for me notwithstanding the pronouncements of distinguished commentators, would accelerate the demise of the present political structure of Confederation. For reasons explained in Chapter 9, Robert Bourassa seemed to be the man capable of seizing the once-in-a-lifetime opportunity that Clio, the muse of history, was about to let fall on his lap. A new political momentum was about to emerge.

One cannot understand the present context and the basic roots of the Quebec/Canada conundrum without a voyage in the past. The *Quiet Resolution* is the ultimate stage of the Quiet Revolution.

The chapter on the Meech Lake Accord was the only one needing significant updating. The two months following publication in French have all but confirmed the surrealistic nature of Canadian federalism. The new section is indicated as such in the text. In the rest of the book, tenses have been left as they were in the original French text.

The essay closes with a peek into the near future. It is not meant to be taken literally but to illustrate the probable and *rational* outcome of the current impasse. In fact, the last three weeks of the Meech Lake roadshow have only added to the plausibility of this scenario. I may add that retrospectively it seems rather tame compared with the unraveling of the Meech II Accord in the middle of June 1990, which very few people would have thought possible. Reality is often stranger and richer than fiction!

It is all the more amusing to see English-Canadian columnists going round in circles, trying to hide their inability to grapple with the nexus of the Canadian Problem. They do not hesitate one minute to condemn Soviet intransigence towards Lithuania, but who is suggesting that Canada should be offering a new deal, a *really* new deal, to Quebec? Very, very few, it seems. But is it so difficult to apply logic to public affairs? To those who judge Quebec's present political integration in Canada to be a good thing for Quebec, one can only put this question: Why not propose the same degree of political integration between Canada and the United States? Why not indeed? The only logic here seems to be the logic of the status quo.

But these are exhilarating times. The European revolution of 1989 is giving birth to a new situation in which we will see, among other developments, the disintegration of a few multinational federations. Canadians will take notice, sooner or later, and come to understand that they too can benefit from the Quiet Resolution. After all, a strong Canada and a strong Quebec in partnership seem preferable to the Canada that now exists.

Foreword

"Je m'envolais vers l'Orient
compliqué avec des idées simples."

"I was flying to the complex
Orient with simple ideas in
mind."

CHARLES DE GAULLE

Yes, the world is ruled by simple ideas. One believes in God, or one doesn't. One believes or does not that others must share one's ideas. Religion, as well as politics and economics, revolves around a few simple ideas...but not simplistic ones.

The concrete application of a simple idea often turns out to be very complex. Democracy is a much simpler idea than the divine right of kings. "All human beings are born free and enjoy equal rights." What could be simpler than that? Yet how much suffering and how many deaths have marked, and still do, the long and winding road leading from the reign of arbitrariness to the rule of law founded on individual rights? And, even in free countries, the daily exercise of democracy is not without occasional violence.

As an idea, the right of nations to determine their own destiny is simpler than imperialism. But when History brings different people together on the same territory, this simple idea becomes a headache and its application can cause as many problems as it solves. Those who preach the abolition of History ("let's make a clean sweep of the past") are often caught up in it.

There are, however, luminous periods when simple ideas faultlessly reassert themselves. The revolution of 1989, in that part of Europe east of the barbed wire, resulted from the meeting of two simple ideas: the failure of communism and the desire for national independence. Yet in 1987, it all seemed terribly complicated.

By one of those sweet coincidences of History, the winds of simple ideas are also blowing on this land of ours. After thirty years of cacophony and hesitation, the different members of the Quebec orchestra are tuning up and getting ready to play the same score together. It will all seem so simple...

Let us then raise the curtain on Quebec, the French land in America.

CHAPTER 1

June 1960

History did not grind to a halt in Quebec and Canada on the evening of May 20, 1980, when the results of the Quebec referendum were announced. Nor did it stop on April 17, 1982, with the proclamation of the new Canadian constitution, even though its authors assumed their work would stand the test of time. An unstable decade with more than its share of surprises has focused nonetheless on certain constants and deadlocked this odd couple of Quebec and Canada. The spouse may extricate herself by deciding on separate bedrooms.

Just as the assassination of Archduke Franz Ferdinand in Sarajevo, at the end of June 1914, started the fateful countdown to World War I, the failure of the Meech Lake Accord provides the opportunity for lancing the abscess that has been poisoning public life in Quebec and Canada. Once the clock starts ticking we are all of us, actors in a drama whose dynamic thrust and outcome no one controls.

Politicians react like everyone else in any given situation. Marketing being the heart of politics in a democracy, it would be wrong to exaggerate the importance of political statements while ignoring the context and the broad strategy of the actors. Quebec is small and reporters overburdened, so that ridiculous statements may get by without anyone noticing. However, it is a consolation to think that the same thing happens in other democratic countries such as France, Great Britain, and particularly the United States. There is no need to feel ashamed of the inconsistencies or the ignorance that have characterized discussion of public issues like the Free Trade Agreement and the Meech Lake Accord. A discordant debate is better than none at all.

However, if we are to understand why it is that, at the beginning of the nineties, a country envied the world over is ready to put itself in question and undergo profound transformations, then we must methodically set out the most important pieces of the puzzle.

From One Nationalism To Another

The eighties began with the referendum campaign. It was, and was meant to be, the logical conclusion of the Quiet Revolution, whose onset is identified with the election of Jean Lesage and the Liberal Party on June 22, 1960, but which should properly be dated the day Paul Sauvé succeeded Premier Maurice Duplessis. No political observer at the time gave Jean Lesage any chance at all of winning an election against Paul Sauvé.[1] However, Sauvé's unexpected death on January 1, 1960, after only 110 days in office, opened the way for Jean Lesage and his party. Their victory was not spectacular: even in 1960, a majority of francophones voted in favour of the Union Nationale.[2]

As soon as the defensive and conservative nationalism of Maurice Duplessis was dead and buried, the decisions and claims of Quebec assumed a new tone. What was the Quiet Revolution if not an uninterrupted affirmation that Quebec, the heart of the French-Canadian nation (as people called it at the time), must possess the institutions and policies necessary for success in the contemporary world? In other words, Duplessis was blamed not for his nationalism but for his outdated vision of the nation. The times called for a modern nationalism. It was seasoned for effect with a national liberation vocabulary, very popular in the early sixties among African colonies on the way to independence.

Pierre Elliott Trudeau, the left-wing intellectual who had been part of the anti-Duplessis struggle, was soon irritated by the turn of events, although they themselves were not surprising. Quebec had fallen seriously behind in education, health care, and authority over its economy. If Quebec was not a colony from the economic point of view, what was it, then? Francophones controlled no large manufacturing firm and were considered second-rate citizens in non-francophone companies, as the *Report of the Royal Commission on Bilingualism and Biculturalism* confirmed a few years later.[3]

As a result of liberal (in the European sense) rather than Keynesian management, Maurice Duplessis had left public finances in a very healthy state, providing the new government with considerable leeway for budget expenditures. However, to deal with Quebec's backwardness and the growing number of young people — the first generation of the baby boom, the tip of the iceberg, was only thirteen or fourteen years old — there was barely enough, considering that the Lesage government was not going to skimp on anything.

The realization of Quebec's backwardness was bound to lead the new government much further than could have been anticipated by the reformist election program the Liberals had submitted to the voters in June 1960. Very soon, the state emerged as the only institution with enough muscle to resolve the problem facing Quebec society, which was to overturn the obstacles perpetuating the social and economic dependence of francophones. Within a few months, the laissez-faire ideology, dominant from 1945 to 1960, gave way to an activism that was all the more energetic because the Government of Quebec was also one of the very few socio-economic institutions controlled by francophones. What pressure there was for change was inevitably exerted on the provincial state.

No society can move one day to the next from compliance to defiance, from faith to skepticism, from alienation to lucidity. There are always people in the vanguard propounding ideas that are first seen as unorthodox. If these ideas reflect the underlying trends of society, they become established truths. John Maynard Keynes was a heretic in 1936 when he published his *General Theory* and laid the foundations of state involvement in macroeconomic regulation. Simone de Beauvoir was a heretic in 1949 when she published *The Second Sex,* which laid bare the mechanisms perpetuating women's social inferiority.

In Quebec, many groups were already at work in the 1950s undermining the society identified with Maurice Duplessis. Once the bolt had been loosened at the top, relations between the top and the bottom took on a new character.

A Very Simple Idea: Political Independence

The notion that the state would build a new society in Quebec led inescapably to the idea of political independence. The descendants of the ten thousand French settlers who came to New France have always been conscious of forming a community that was different from the American colonies and, later, from other Canadian provinces. It was distinctive in language, culture, and history. Yet the Canadian government gave little recognition to this specific character as regards, for instance, francophone presence in the public service and in Crown corporations, the language of work in these institutions and of services delivered to the population. Pierre Trudeau explained francophone dissatisfaction with the federal government very well: "In the past, the Department of External Affairs has built up an image of Canada as a unilingual, English country. I could almost say the same of other departments and Crown corporations. The federal capital is an English capital."[4]

Decolonization in Africa being one of the leading issues at the end of the fifties, the idea of independence was in the air. But why did it flourish so late in Quebec? The Tremblay Commission, created by Maurice Duplessis in 1953 to look into the constitutional question, noted in its final report in 1956 that none of the 250 briefs submitted advanced the idea of sovereignty.[5] Why not?

Many explanations are possible. The most important one is that the groups most likely to promote the idea of sovereignty (intellectuals, union leaders, and the like) were those most resolutely opposed to Duplessis: the idea of an independent Quebec headed by Duplessis made their blood run cold. They naturally looked to Ottawa to escape the arbitrary nature of his rule. Before even thinking of independence, there had to be a decent government in Quebec.

Moreover, in the fifties, the whole Western world *seemed* to be moving away from assertive nationalism. Wasn't it in 1957 that the Treaty of Rome was signed, creating the European Economic Community, the first step in a long march to the United States of Europe? Didn't the Keynesian revolution require a more centralized approach to economic policy? An economist at Laval University, Maurice Lamontagne, used to preach along those lines, proposing a significant transfer of power from the provinces to the federal government.[6] In the same vein, didn't the appearance of the welfare state require the expansion of central governments, the only institutions with the resources to provide nationwide social security programs? In a federal system, this supposed that federal power would grow at the expense of the provinces. In this context, a provincialist such as Maurice Duplessis was at odds with his own time.

Everything changed with the advent of Jean Lesage and the Liberals, particularly the way of looking at relations between Quebec and Ottawa. The passivity of the past was replaced by a desire to take the offensive. An observer, having left Quebec before June 1960 and returning four or five years later, would have stared in disbelief. Beginning in

1964–65, every claim put forward by Quebec was a body blow against the kind of federalism practised on the other side of the Ottawa River.

Quebec's demands escalated in accordance with the idea of independence, which was enjoying great media success. In fact, Jean Lesage involuntarily promoted separatist movements. They simply projected his policies to their logical conclusion: if it was to Quebec's advantage to recover this or that constitutional power in the name of the Quebec nation, then why not recover all of them? Jean Lesage found himself between a rock and a hard place. Should he and Ottawa come to an agreement that did not fully meet Quebec's aspirations, he would be disavowed by public opinion, as happened in the case of the Fulton-Favreau constitutional formula.* Yet if he obtained major concessions from the federal government, it would merely whet the appetite of the nationalist opposition, which could always accuse him of selling out too cheaply. Independently of Jean Lesage's federalist convictions, his opposition to excessive subordination to the federal government served to stimulate national affirmation.

At least one federalist thought it might be dangerous for the federal government to give away too much: Pierre Trudeau.

The Advent of Pierre Trudeau

The federal election of April 1963 brought to power a Liberal minority government led by Lester Pearson. One of his priorities was to formulate a clear response to the growing demands of Quebec and to differentiate the Liberals from John Diefenbaker's Conservatives and their idea of "an unhyphenated Canadian nation."

* This formula would have permitted, among other things, the federal government to extend its jurisdictions insofar as seven provinces representing half the Canadian population agreed.

Pearson's policy of sympathy and harmony came to be known as cooperative federalism. It led, in 1963, to the establishment of the Royal Commission on Bilingualism and Biculturalism. It also led to the recognition of the provinces' right to withdraw from joint programs, a right Quebec was the only one to exercise. It led, finally, to the recognition of the Quebec Pension Plan, which would coexist with the Canada Pension Plan supported by all of the other provinces.

During this transition period, Pierre Trudeau was a political loner. He had distanced himself from the provincial Liberals, who had become too nationalist. Already, in 1962, he had challenged the usefulness of nationalizing the private power companies, although he agreed not to be too vocal in his opposition.[7] He dismissed outright all of the constitutional pretensions of Jean Lesage, who had persuaded Pearson to give in on the question of the Canada Pension Plan. The establishment of the Quebec Pension Plan, in 1965, went together with the foundation of the Caisse de dépôt et placement, whose mandate was to administer contributions to the pension plan on the basis of two criteria: sound management *and* Quebec's economic development.

Pierre Trudeau's policy views were of little consequence at the time. He was still only teaching law and writing with a scathing pen. The Liberal Party of Canada had refused, not without reason, to accept him in its ranks at the time of the general election of 1963: he had copiously insulted Pearson in the pages of *Cité Libre.* * Because of his views, however, he acquired a certain notoriety among intellectuals in English Canada.

As early as 1962, René Lévesque, minister of natural resources in the Lesage government, and this aloof intellectual, who took pleasure in provoking his anger, were ideologically estranged. The seeds of the two fundamental options facing Quebec were germinating in the ground.

Pearson had little choice after the political events that

* A periodical edited by Pierre Trudeau and Gérard Pelletier during the fifties and early sixties and devoted to an anti-Duplessis conception of Quebec society.

shook Ottawa in the wake of the election of April 1963. On one hand, political "scandals" removed leading Quebec figures from the government, notably Maurice Lamontagne and Guy Favreau. On the other, the political initiative was clearly in Quebec rather than in Ottawa, which could only react to the steady bombardment from Quebec. Pearson was badly in need of a new Quebec team: he found a ready-made star in Jean Marchand, president of the Confédération des syndicats nationaux, the Confederation of National Trade Unions. Marchand was then at the height of his fame, and Pearson already saw him as his own successor. Gérard Pelletier, former editor-in-chief of *La Presse,* was also ready to make the jump into national politics. But there was a third musketeer: Pierre Trudeau. In 1965, Pearson finally accepted him. Ironically, of the three so-called doves, Trudeau was the only one given an absolutely safe riding.

Pierre Trudeau entered politics with the idea of arresting the decline of federal power and prestige in Quebec and making the federal government and all of Canada more accommodating to the French Fact. For Canada should also be the country of French-Canadians and they should feel at home everywhere in it. As de Gaulle said in other circumstances: "Quite a vast program!"

Seventeen years of constitutional battles were about to begin.

A Constitutional Reference Chart

Yes, we shall talk about the constitution. The argument of those who favour the status quo, that voters are more interested in bread and butter than in the constitution, was shown to be unfounded during the "patriation" operation of 1980–1982 as well as during the campaign in English Canada against the Meech Lake Accord. True, the public quickly gets bored when no distinctions are made between essential and secondary points; people just yawn when confusion sets in. The constitution of 1867, which created the Canadian federal system, had 147 articles of varying importance.

A constitution expresses the essential elements of a country's political life. How did the civil war between Christians and Moslems get started in Lebanon? The Lebanese constitution of 1947 declared that the president should be Christian and the prime minister a Sunni Moslem. The Shiite Moslems were therefore excluded from the pyramid of power. But today, a more rapid demographic growth has made them numerically the most important Arab group in the country. In Eastern Europe, including the Soviet Union, what was the most insistent demand of opposition groups? It was the repeal of the constitutional clause awarding a monopoly of power to the Communist Party. And by reforming the French constitution in 1959, Charles de Gaulle brought political stability to France.

In Quebec, the interminable constitutional debate has two major axes which can be examined separately because they are in fact independent of each other: language, and the division of powers between the federal government and the provinces. Two general attitudes are possible as regards the first axis or line of force, and three for the second. They can be set out in a little diagram that can help us find our way through the Byzantine web of constitutional conflict in Canada.

The amending formula is obviously a key aspect of the constitution. But is it a major axis in the discussion? It is not necessarily so for our purposes because only recently did it become a contentious issue between Quebec and Ottawa. From 1960 to 1980, everyone believed, or acted as if they did, that Quebec had a veto on any constitutional amendment affecting it.

There are six squares in this diagram. Four of them can easily be identified by means of appropriate political personalities. Two squares are empty, not because the diagram is incoherent but because the Quebec context has not favoured the emergence of these particular options. It is quite possible for a Quebecer to support sovereignty for functional reasons while advocating institutional bilingualism both in Quebec and in Canada. For example, Helsinki, the capital of Finland, is perfectly bilingual (Finnish and Swedish), even though Swedes represent only 15 percent of the population. Conversely, it is possible to advocate total French unilingualism in Quebec without claiming a broader jurisdiction for the provincial government. In fact, the Swiss and Belgian models are built along these lines.

The two empty squares show the absolute primacy of the social and geographic environment.

Within each square, there is room for nuances. There have been many variants of "special status." As the name implies, they propose a major transfer of constitutional power from Ottawa to Quebec regardless of what happens

A Constitutional Reference Chart

Language / Division of Powers	Pancanadian Bilingualism	Quebec:French Ottawa and Fredericton: bilingual Elsewhere: bit of French
Status Quo	1. P. Trudeau	2.
Special Status	3. J. Lesage, D. Johnson, C. Ryan (until 1982)	4. R. Bourassa
Sovereignty	5.	6. R. Lévesque

with the other provinces. In a similar manner, the primacy of French in Quebec and administrative bilingualism in Ottawa and New Brunswick, where 30 percent of the population is French, are also matters of degree. The proponents of this linguistic option have one thing in common: they do not want cross-country bilingualism. Finally, those who support sovereignty don't generally care what happens in Ottawa and in the other provinces with respect to language after independence. Some, however, would like reciprocal arrangements for the protection of linguistic minorities.

The political history of Quebec over the past twenty years is highlighted by three major confrontations: Square 1 against Square 4, Square 4 against Square 6, and Square 1 against Square 6. During the same period, public opinion was gradually moving from Square 3 to Square 4, and, after a pause, now seems ready to jump the fence into Square 6. We must have a closer look at this.

Chapter 2

French Canada's Last Missionary

Pierre Trudeau is one of those rare politicians who have put on paper an articulate vision of the global Canadian picture *before* making the leap into politics. Since he could hardly anticipate, even in the spring of 1965, where destiny would lead him, one may suppose that Trudeau the intellectual expressed his true thoughts in his articles and commentaries. Whoever looks into them will discover that there are inconsistencies between the politician and the intellectual, and not only on issues that would be considered secondary. And if there has been any change in his Canadian view of Quebec, it takes the form of heightened intransigence towards his native province.

The Missionary's Luggage

Judging the division of powers outlined in the constitution of 1867 to be satisfactory for Quebec, and considering in 1965 that the future would favour existing provincial powers,[1] Trudeau rejected Quebec's demand for a special status.* He believed it would incite Quebec to become inward-looking

* In this study, only those of Trudeau's thoughts and works related to the Canadian crisis of 1990 are considered.

and ultimately lead to independence. Accordingly, he urged Quebecers to make full use of provincial powers to build a more prosperous Quebec and a more powerful provincial state, and participate fully in the federal system, something they had not done previously.

To this end, however, it was necessary that francophones feel at home in the federal public service and, as much as possible, in the rest of the country. This presupposed the equality of the two official languages at all levels of the federal government and the recognition of the language and school rights of francophones outside Quebec. And when the time came, these two points would subsequently be incorporated into a renewed constitution. "It would not be very realistic to rely upon good will or purely political action. The reforms I am proposing...must be irrevocably binding upon both the federal and provincial governments."[2]

In this respect, Trudeau was just as radical as any provincial politician. He shared the vision of Jean Lesage and Daniel Johnson. It is therefore not surprising that writers from English Canada, such as Christina McCall-Newman, a specialist of Canadian politics,[3] saw him as a French-Canadian nationalist. After all, he had always expressed a deep admiration for Henri Bourassa.

Daniel Johnson, however, would not discuss constitutional reform without a new division of powers, which in concrete terms meant a special status for Quebec. When Trudeau became justice minister in 1967 and took charge of constitutional negotiations, conflict and failure became unavoidable. But the minister of justice was not too concerned, since he did not think the status quo was untenable.

Meanwhile, in Quebec, linguistic fever was mounting. The government would soon be overwhelmed.

Speak White*

Francophones in Quebec obviously wished for more

* Title of a now famous poem by Michèle Lalonde

open-mindedness in Ottawa. They also felt a natural sympathy for survivors of the French-Canadian diaspora on whose behalf they pleaded for more cultural oxygen. However, one would have to be very poorly informed to imagine that this sympathy would take precedence over their own problems in Quebec. These were illustrated in the discreet campaign of private power utilities against impending nationalization, the issue of the 1962 referendum-like election. They implied that francophones were not competent to manage power utilities and that the introduction of French as the language of work in the future Crown corporation was absolutely utopian, a notion shared by a number of francophones.[4]

Trudeau's initial opposition was founded on narrow economic grounds: the capital would be better spent elsewhere while nationalization would only fuel nationalist conceit. He did not recognize that a decision based on national considerations might be socially beneficial. Even in strict economic terms his reasoning was rather shaky: if an investment seems worthwhile and no local investors are ready to come forward, then state intervention is quite justified. Judging by subsequent developments, nationalization was a resounding success from every point of view: economic, social, and linguistic, in spite of Hydro-Québec's recent problems.

There is an intriguing paradox here. Trudeau recognized that French Canadians in Quebec were victims of discrimination on the job market, and he wanted provincial authorities to move against it: "in all levels of industry, from the very top down to the foreman, French Canadians have been poorly represented in proportion to their number. It even happens that a Quebec worker being hired for industry is required to speak English as well as French — a form of discrimination that should be rigorously forbidden by Quebec law."[5]

The problem was later compounded by the prospect of a decline in the relative number and influence of francophones in the Montreal area as a result of the massive integration of immigrants into the anglophone community.[6] Newcomers, who were then free to choose the language of education for their children, overwhelmingly chose English-language schools. The choice was perfectly reasonable, particularly as non-Catholics were not admitted to Catholic schools, which were virtually the only public French-language schools. However, the idea that the fate of French was being decided in the educational system and in the Montreal business world prevailed after much discussion. Much discussion indeed.

For many people were apprehensive at the thought that Quebec might legislate on language, even though the language of work and access to the school system were solely within provincial jurisdiction, with the exception of federal government services and federally chartered companies. In the other provinces, immigrants had no right to French schools — which did not worry them unduly! The economic and political weight of Quebec's anglophone community had a lot to do with the generally laissez-faire attitude of Quebec élites. At the end of the 1960s, this community had but one slogan: *Speak White.*

A commonly held view was that francophones in Montreal, and even all of Quebec, should learn English for economic success: it was "the language of business, of world trade, and of technology." Wasn't it the responsibility of Canada's francophone minority to adapt to the rest of the continent? Richard Joy, who pioneered linguistic demography in Canada, had shown that the French language was regressing everywhere else in the country.[7] No wonder that, in November 1969, Bill 63 had to impose the teaching of French as a second language in English-language schools in Quebec. In every other respect, however, the law preserved complete linguistic freedom.

Nevertheless, the anthem of persuasion was chanted in every tone for many years. Precious time was lost pleading for elementary concessions which never came graciously: collective agreements in French, minimal bilingualism in commercial signs, and so on. It was finally evident that complete linguistic freedom did not work. The only alternative for improving the status and prestige of French in Quebec was legislation.

Ironically, Ottawa was the first to use legislation to redress linguistic inequalities.

The First Skirmishes

The future prime minister of Canada did not accept, contrary to what he wrote before his entry into federal politics, that the people of Quebec could use state power if necessary to impose the French language in Quebec, particularly on immigrants.

What was the first law to impose the use of a language anywhere in Canada? It was the Official Languages Act, adopted by the Canadian Parliament in 1969, the first major piece of legislation of the reign of Pierre Trudeau. It introduced official bilingualism in the federal public service, in the national capital and across the country, wherever justified by the number of francophones or anglophones.

At first, the idea was simply to restore some sort of balance between anglophones and francophones who were seriously underrepresented in the federal public service. However, civil servants soon became aware that the most interesting positions were awarded to bilingual people and hence to francophones. To forestall a rebellion in English Canada, it became necessary to transform unilingual civil servants into bilingual ones. Anglophones would therefore take French lessons during working hours, at the expense of anglophone *and* francophone taxpayers.[8]

Some competent civil servants are not gifted for languages, while others who are might be mediocre administrators. Learning a second language at forty or fifty is no easy task, particularly if it is not used every day. But no matter, bilingualism was to be a criterion for advancement, and the whole public service was transformed into one vast language laboratory. A large number of public servants endured serious disruptions in their lives; some were seeing their career opportunities restricted in a way that had never been anticipated at the time of their appointment.

How could the promoter of such a law be so hostile to Bill 22 and Bill 101, passed by the Quebec National Assembly in July 1974 and August 1977? These two laws had an effect comparable to that of the Official Languages Act on the daily operations of firms and individuals. In education, the two laws scrupulously upheld acquired rights and took nothing away from anyone already residing in Quebec.

The only possible explanation is that Trudeau opposed the ultimate goals of these laws.

Bill 22 had three objectives. The first was to make French the sole official language of Quebec outside the courts and the National Assembly, whose bilingual character was entrenched in the Canadian constitution. French was mandatory in government contracts, although English remained optional. Consumers and workers could demand French-language contracts. Affirmation of the predominance of the French language was expected to impose its use in the workplace gradually.

Francophones in Quebec subscribed to this objective, part of the Quebec Liberal Party program since *1966.*[9] They wouldn't accept in their own house the burden of total bilingualism, which could only be detrimental to them, particularly in the higher reaches of the business world. Obviously, a knowledge of both languages was necessary in certain positions, and this was generally accepted.

The objective was to turn the page on a period when any francophone had to be sufficiently bilingual for rewarding positions in business, while anglophones were spared this requirement, even if they were in regular contact with consumers or worked in the public service. Unilingual anglophones were actually employed in the provincial public service as well as the federal one. Everyone knows how things work out in this type of situation: in the presence of an anglophone, francophones spoke English to each other. In certain sections of the social affairs ministry in Quebec City, the practice continued until 1976.

The second objective written into Bill 22 was to restrict immigrants' access to English-language schools, which henceforth would accept only students with an adequate knowledge of English. The third objective was to give more prominence to the French character of Quebec. To this end, public signs, posters, and billboards had to be in French, but without restricting the use of an accompanying language.

From today's perspective, this first language law with teeth (in Quebec) seems rather innocuous. However, to understand how language politics became more radical three years later and the context giving rise to Bill 178 in 1988, it is necessary to recall how Bill 22 was greeted in Quebec by anglophones and a sizable proportion of allophones (people whose first language is other than English or French).

A rereading of the English-language press of the day gives the impression of a police state in Quebec. Robert Bourassa was a "fascist," and this was just one of the portrayals, and not the most extreme by any means, of the promoter of Bill 22. Quebec anglophones saw themselves as Canadians, that's all. And here were the French forcing their language down their throats!

Two contemporary reactions should be noted. The first was collective. Montreal anglophones circulated a petition denouncing Bill 22, particularly its requirement that all public signs include French. There were then some one and a half million people in Quebec who were not French, including the very young and the elderly. Does anyone today remember how many signatures there were on the petition? Many will be flabbergasted by the answer: *600,000.* William

Tetley was the cabinet minister responsible for explaining the law to the English community.* His name was mud. However, since 1977, he takes a certain pleasure in recalling how this gut opposition to Bill 22 suddenly evaporated when Bill 101, a more robust piece of legislation, was tabled in the National Assembly. Overnight, Bill 22 became "*a very reasonable piece of legislation.*"

The second noteworthy reaction was that of Pierre Trudeau. Bill 22 is politically stupid, was in essence what he said. Obviously, Quebecers were isolated on their reserve. How could they count on any support in English Canada if even their own federal leaders lashed out at them?

One of the most persistent myths of Quebec's political history is that the defection of the anglophone vote in the wake of Bill 22 brought down Premier Bourassa's government in the elections of 1976. In fact close analysis shows that the Parti Québécois would have had a slim majority of seats even if the Liberals had received their usual anglophone vote.

Realism and Utopia

The Quebec perspective clashed with Pierre Trudeau's Canadian vision, as expressed in the package of language rights he planned to incorporate into the Victoria Charter of 1971. The intention was to confirm the constitutional equality of English and French across Canada, that is, in each of the provinces. Most of the provinces were very reluctant, if not hostile. As usual, the government of Quebec had gone furthest to accommodate the federal proposal, even if it rejected freedom of choice in the language of education and total linguistic equality within the province.[10]

---

* William Tetley, in the spring of 1989, speaking before ACFAS (Association canadienne française pour l'avancement des sciences), a French-language cultural and scientific organization, recalled this episode in a talk on Bill 178. The director of one of the organizations responsible for administering the language legislation, who was present, could not believe his ears and confessed that he could not recall this incident. He is not the only one.

The Victoria conference failed because of disagreement between Ottawa and Quebec over shared jurisdiction of social affairs.

The clashing language perspectives of Bourassa and Trudeau had little to do with the way the proponents of a French Quebec viewed the political future, their position was not incompatible *in itself* with orthodox federalism. When Gérard Pelletier, for example, said that "Quebec should be as French as Ontario is English," was he questioning the very existence of Canada? Not at all. Eight of the ten provinces had then only one official language, hence Bill 22 *theoretically* placed Quebec in tune with these eight provinces. In fact, anglophones in Quebec would continue to benefit from all reasonable services in their own language.

Today, Gérard Pelletier's little phrase seems trite. Yet it goes much further than Bill 101. It is not clear whether its author was aware of the consequences: very heavy constraints would have been and would still be necessary to bring about such a situation, since the economic influence and geographical distribution of Ontario's francophones are hardly comparable to that of Quebec's anglophones. But one can see the direction taken by Pelletier's thoughts.

Even orthodox federalists on the provincial scene were subject to Trudeau's outbursts, and that was because his conception of federalism, as it relates to language, had nothing orthodox about it. He could hardly claim (and did not wish to) that Quebec anglophones should enjoy more rights than francophones outside Quebec, even if this would be consistent with the idea of providing services wherever justified by numbers. Accordingly, the only other possibility was the promotion of the idea of a bilingual Canada from coast to coast. The provinces were more or less encouraged to imitate the federal government, which was ready to pay the costs. Quebec's language laws were the untoward event that upset Trudeau's vision. But they did not upset reality.

Language and Demography in Canada

Journalist Peter Brimelow recalls in his book on Canada that Winston Churchill insisted that his advisers during World War II summarize the main elements of any situation, no matter how complex, on half a sheet of paper.[11] Canada's situation, with respect to linguistic demography, lends itself to this kind of exercise.

Demography is at the heart of the destiny of Quebec—and of Canada's problem.

French Quebec constitutes 21 percent of the Canadian population and 83 percent of that of Quebec. If one takes language of the home as a criterion, a more relevant one than first language, then 90 percent of all French-speaking Canadians live in Quebec. This is to say that, outside Quebec, francophones represent marginal groups, except along the border that separates Quebec and Ontario and in Acadia. The decline of these communities is tangible everywhere except in Acadia, the homeland of la Sagouine,[12] and results from a process Trudeau has diplomatically described as "cultural osmosis."

If French Canadians, one quarter of the total population, were distributed *uniformly* across the country, they would represent an important minority in each province with very little collective influence. Few French-Canadians would be elected to Parliament because the English-speaking majority would have little reason to make any concessions to the French-speaking minority. On the basis of this scenario, total assimilation would be well under way. If, on the other hand, French Quebec had twice its present population, genuine equality would be inevitable within federal institutions, not only in language and official recognition but also in public policy. And this would happen even if not a single French-speaking person lived outside Quebec and the national capital.

The source of the Canadian problem can therefore be found in the concentration of French-speaking people nationally and their relative importance within Quebec. The combination of these two percentages (21 percent and 83 percent) is fundamental. Reduce the first figure by half and Quebec is just a little province among others, unable to compete for a hearing in the whole of Canada, even if its population were almost entirely francophone. Cut the second percentage by a dozen points or so, and then Quebec's French character would be much less obvious. In such a case, Montreal would have a small English-speaking majority, something that would upset the whole demographic, linguistic, and political balance. Bill 101, as we know it, would have been impossible in such a context.

Therefore, 21 percent and 83 percent, as of *today*. The first figure has been falling for thirty years; the trend cannot be reversed because of the influx of immigrants into Ontario and western Canada. The second figure has been stationary since 1986 (after rising for a decade), and may even be declining because of the recent upturn in immigration, legal and illegal, into Quebec.[13] These are the two fundamental and complementary constraints Quebec must face, and no amount of bombast will cause them to go away. By the same token, it will be impossible to reverse the course of history for the French-language communities scattered across Canada, vestiges of an era that never managed to assume the shape of the Canadian dream cherished by generations of French-Canadians. (After 1867 they believed the Canadian west would be open to their language and culture.) West of Quebec, the rate of assimilation, based on the ratio of the population whose home language is French and the population of French origin, is higher than 65 percent.

A few basic conclusions follow from these considerations. The numerical inferiority of francophones in Canada makes it impossible ever to achieve real linguistic equality between francophones and anglophones, even at the federal level. Success would depend on the constant tyranny of the minority—or the establishment in each government department of airtight language sections, with all the daily translation problems this implies. We would be poles apart from the current notion of Canadian bilingualism.

And, even if it were so, bilingualism would always be necessary for a francophone who wants access to the upper reaches of the Canadian public or parapublic service, while an anglophone could be unilingual. How many positions today, officially classified as bilingual, are in fact held by people who are practically unilingual! But almost all those who were identified with French Power in Ottawa were perfectly bilingual.

Let it be understood that this analysis is a dispassionate exercise. It is not a litany of grievances. No law can modify this basic reality; it can only make things a bit more palatable for francophones, many of whom recognize the constraints inherent in their demographic inequality.

They might have been better disposed to recognize it had the federal government accepted the necessity and urgency of the linguistic transformation in Quebec, and had it been aware of a dual French Power in the making, proceeding from the same mutation, one in Quebec and the other in Ottawa: the battle for French had to be waged on both fronts. With such an approach, the call for excellence, which is at the root of Pierre Trudeau's thinking, would have seemed more coherent and tempting.

However, twenty years of agitation in favour of total bilingualism at the institutional level have raised unrealistic expectations. According to a 1983 survey by the Treasury Board, 83 percent of francophone civil servants were anxious to use more French in their work. The problem did not arise in Quebec but in the national capital![14] In Quebec, it was actually possible to work almost exclusively in French.

The survey shows that francophones are able to work in English; the opposite is quite rare, even in 1990. "The language of work in the Public Service is still, to an overwhelming extent, English, even in institutions with a critical mass of Francophone employees in the 20 percent to 25 percent range."[15]

Elementary Common Sense

Let us return to the Constitutional Reference Chart on page 10. Bill 22 and, three years later, Bill 101, reflected the shift of public opinion from Square 3 to Square 4. A majority of federalists supported Bill 101 which, shorn of its anticonstitutional clauses, was perfectly compatible with the federal system. It can even be claimed that Bill 101 consolidated federalism in Quebec for a while.

The two laws reflect a binational or territorial conception of Canada and realistically transcribe the country's character onto paper. On the one hand, according to this conception, the federal government must effectively practise institutional bilingualism, creating a limited number of bilingual positions, so as to provide services in both official languages wherever justified by numbers. On the other hand, there are eight English provinces, one French, and one officially bilingual, New Brunswick. The money thus saved could have been used to assist the more viable French minorities outside Quebec *and* support French culture within Quebec.

This was, as seen from Quebec, the sensible way of dealing with the language issue in Canada (the division of powers between Ottawa and the provinces, particularly Quebec, was a different issue but just as conflict-ridden). The majority in Quebec were not asking for more, nor did they hope for more. They knew very well that the language and school confrontations of francophones outside Quebec, except for Acadia and a few Franco-Ontarian communities, were the last battles in a war already lost.

For the proponents of a *single* Canadian nation, the territorial vision was still anathema. It opens the door to balkanization and the eventual separation of Quebec. The argument is not without merit when it focuses on the traditional demands of Quebec about the division of powers. But it is hard to see how Pierre Trudeau's linguistic utopia is a better cement for Canada than common sense. It is an either/or proposition. Either Canada is of economic and political interest to Quebec, in which case the way of linguistic common sense will help preserve federal ties, or Canada has nothing of value to offer Quebec, in which case total bilingualism in the federal public service and wide-ranging concessions to francophone minorities outside Quebec will be of no consequence at all.

In fact, Trudeau's linguistic utopia concealed, as do all utopias, a fatal danger. Reality would eventually reassert itself and, in doing so, provoke a backlash all the more irrational for having been suppressed for so long and all the more passionate because of Quebec's own linguistic path. It was forseeable that Quebec would have no hesitation in pursuing its linguistic destiny. The blind resentment against Quebec, which has infected parts of English Canada since the beginning of 1990, shows that this is not vain speculation.

Meanwhile, twenty-two years have been lost in illusory pursuits. So much money and effort for such a bitter harvest!

A New Religion

In 1968, English Canada believed Pierre Trudeau was a gift from the gods to counter the rise of separatism in Quebec. Pushing the public service towards a linguistic utopia seemed a small price to pay for Canadian unity. Bilingualism was to be the alpha and omega of Canadian policy. Pierre Trudeau was to be the last missionary from French Canada and the ultimate metamorphosis of the *revanche des berceaux*, the Cradle's Revenge, as the explosive demographic growth of French Canada used to be called. Prodded by Trudeau, Canada was moving towards complete language equality, something only a truly phenomenal *revanche des berceaux* could have brought about.

The term *missionary* is doubly apt for Pierre Trudeau.

First, bilingualism was for him an article of faith, and any doubt expressed about it was considered heretical, as Richard Gwyn has pointed out.[16] Secondly, anglophones outside Quebec were not the only ones to have qualms about this new religion whose rituals were coming out of the shadows. Francophones in Quebec had never been very fervent, and Trudeau knew that. But he thought he might convert them to the true faith. Indeed, in this respect, most Canadians were still pagans.

The proof of Trudeau's awareness of failing support is that he never dared challenge Quebec directly on the language issue. He could be insulting ("Bill 101 is a return to the Middle Ages")[17] but he would never invoke his considerable powers. The means were not lacking: he could have withheld federal funds from Quebec or resurrected the power to disallow provincial laws, still inscribed in the constitution but fallen into disuse. He did nothing for a very simple reason: he had no chance of winning such a confrontation. Trudeau, however, knew how to recycle defeat: at the outset of the referendum campaign, he argued that Quebec within Canada could be just as French as Ontario was English![18] (The least one can say is that it wasn't thanks to him.)

During the last stages of negotiations on the patriation of the constitution, in November 1981, he had the opportunity to break the main clauses of Bill 101 (restricted access to English-language schools and French as the sole official language). Yet all he did was impose the Canada clause in place of the Quebec clause concerning access to English-language schools, a minor modification that the government of Quebec did not oppose in principle.* Had he chosen confrontation over Bill 101, he would have triggered a massive political revolt in Quebec.

This new religion of bilingualism was not the price to be paid for Canadian unity. The referendum results confirmed this anew. But that did not mean Quebec's path of common

* Children of parents educated in English in Canada (not just in Quebec) would have access to English schools in Quebec.

sense in linguistic matters would have been accepted without a fight.

This path, in 1968, did not run parallel with that of English Canada. The proponents of the Canadian nation saw a majority and a minority, both *Canadian.* Common sense in English Canada suggested the recognition of legitimate rights of the minority with regard to its own language in the federal public service and access to services in its own language in areas where it was numerically strong enough.

However, a unilingual *French* province was a heretical notion. No distinction could be made between anglophones living in different provinces, and those who happened to live in Quebec had exactly the same rights as all the others since they belonged to the Canadian majority. Moreover, the French minority did not have the right to prevent immigrants from integrating into the Canadian majority. Accordingly, Canada was composed of a somewhat bilingual central government, two provinces subject to bilingualism, and eight unilingual provinces.

Two conceptions, each based on common sense, might have confronted each other. History cannot be undone, to be sure, but it would certainly have been easier to reconcile these two conceptions, both sticking close to reality, than to carry out Pierre Trudeau's project. On the one hand, nothing could prevent Quebec from resorting to forced imposition of French. On the other hand, Quebec's political weight guaranteed that a moderately high level of bilingualism would eventually prevail in the public and parapublic service in the national capital. After understanding that Quebec claims did not go any further on the language front, English Canada sooner or later would have accepted this territorial vision of Canada.

History can sometimes offer minor pleasures and sometimes great happiness, as in 1989 in Eastern Europe. It may sometimes inflict small or great unhappiness upon us. In the former category, there is the premature death of André Laurendeau, the co-chairman of the Royal Commission on Bilingualism and Biculturalism, in 1968. It deprived us of the expected last volume of the Commission's report, which was to deal with constitutional problems and Quebec's role as a distinct society.

We know that André Laurendeau attached great importance to the status of French as a working language, not only in the federal public service but in Quebec as well.[19] He believed that the Canadian government could play an active role in this respect. His vision clashed with that of Pierre Trudeau, who eventually dissociated himself from the recommendations of the Laurendeau-Dunton Commission on some essential points. But let us close this nostalgic aside.

The two common-sense visions had some points in common. One was accepting the fate of francophone minorities outside Quebec.

Ode to the Ghetto

Quebec's language laws, the Canadian government's Official Languages Act, and assistance to French minorities outside Quebec emanated from the same principle: the necessity for lawmakers to correct the natural evolution that was deemed to be negative. An economist would say that political power was used to obtain something not allowed by the free play of market forces. It is, in fact, the very argument Trudeau used to condemn the nationalists in Quebec: "If you had any proficiency in such and such a field you would never need artificial protection."

Why wasn't this Ode to Excellence sung to federal civil servants and to francophone minorities? Apart from obvious ideological reasons, based on the desire to transform Canada into a bilingual half-continent, it is hard to say why. However, it has brought about such stupendous incoherence that one is surprised to hear it used again nowadays.

Thus it is that, for certain people, wanting Quebec to be

as French as possible means retreating into a ghetto. (But does one hear about a Danish or Swedish ghetto?) When the argument is put forward by an Anglo-Canadian or by an American, it is easy to see its origins even while challenging its relevance: it is a matter of accepting the supremacy of the English (or American) language, which supposedly represents the thrust of History. But when it is heard from a Trudeauite, one can't help smiling. Wanting to live in French, study in French, relax, and even work in French in Regina or St. John's, swamped by English — isn't this the real ghetto?

The commissioner of official languages does not hesitate to avail himself of the arguments of French lobbies outside Quebec, who maintain that French schools and French immersion represent two different and even antagonistic ideas.[20] In other words, apartheid is necessary for the survival of this frail flower of French culture west of Ottawa and east of Quebec. But to recognize its frailty is to admit, without actually saying so, that its life is being artificially prolonged from outside: French culture outside Quebec, save for Acadia, is connected to a respirator.

What do francophones outside Quebec do if they really want to live and succeed in French? They move to Quebec. Gabrielle Roy, Jean Éthier-Blais, Daniel Lavoie, Édith Butler, and Antonine Maillet, all have at least one point in common: born in francophone enclaves, they have made their homes and achieved stardom in Quebec. They are not the only ones. Quebec, and France as well, has made it possible for them to live from their talents. Similarly, Quebec writers, composers and performers who want to exert some influence or have a hearing beyond Quebec must tackle the French market.

It would be preferable to recognize that assimilation is inevitable for all these little enclaves rather than pretend that some miracle will bring about their resurrection. In fact, current aid allows them to soften the harshest aspects of assimilation. However, in the midst of a budget crisis, this may be questionable. But old dreams die hard. There are still commentators who occasionally stifle a sob for the French of Gravelbourg or the Acadians of Prince Edward Island. For some reason, they don't do it for Lowell, Massachusetts, or Manchester, New Hampshire, even though New England is close by and St. Boniface at the end of the world.

Where is the politician who will have the courage to say, "Let's stop whining. All federal aid to French minorities should be concentrated on the few communities who have a reasonable chance of survival. But, of course, we encourage the provinces not to be too stingy with their French minorities..."?

It is generally believed in Quebec that all language "extremists" are on the same side of the barricades. But the ideology of bilingualism has promoted unwarranted expectations. Thus: "Francophones outside Quebec will in the future seek official acknowledgements of linguistic duality by all the provincial governments....Since bilingualism has not checked assimilation, what is wanted now is nothing less than services of equal quality....Francophones wish to be able to live in French on a daily basis, and not only 'where numbers warrant'."[21]

Such is the most recent position of the Fédération des Francophones Hors-Québec, put forward in June 1989. This is, of course, an organization supported financially by the federal government. It does not speak for francophones who are moving to Quebec or who have decided to integrate into their present environment in order to live normal lives.

On reading this type of statement, on hearing about the conflicts brought about by public bussing of twenty francophones to this school and thirty to that school, on learning that small communities of francophones refuse to send their children to French immersion classes for reasons that have more to do with the fear of assimilation than the quality of education, one can only conclude that Canada is a country made ill by its minorities and that Quebec is, in effect, better off keeping its distance from these people. Is there any other country in the Western world with such a cult of the *minority label*?

But there is worse.

The media's obsession with language minorities, over all these years, has validated the absolutely extravagant idea that the fate of Canada is somehow linked to the way these minorities are treated. "Canada cannot survive if Quebec becomes entirely French and the rest of Canada exclusively English." This means the future of this rich country of 26 million people rests entirely upon several tens of thousands of dispersed francophones and a few hundreds of thousands of anglophones in Montreal, who resemble those French aristocrats of 1815 who had learnt nothing and forgotten nothing.

How pathetic! How idiotic! To think that no one has ever heard of Belgium or Switzerland. But these people are only Belgian or Swiss. We Canadians had a special calling: according to Pierre Trudeau, we would become a model for all humanity.

This is not the first time that a country has been fragmented by missionaries.

Entering the nineties, one can anticipate the verdict of History. Bill 101 will be recognized as highly successful. The Official Languages Act will be seen as only moderately successful in spite of the huge resources behind it, and the cumulative aid to francophones outside Quebec will be written off as a complete failure with respect to the objectives pursued.

But how did a democratic country get itself into such a fix?

Chapter 3

The Great Misunderstanding

How did Pierre Trudeau's vision, which did not have the support of a majority in Quebec, draw the country into such a mess? The answer is written into the electoral process and the logic of political parties.

In the history of societies, not all moments are equivalent. There are high and low points, revolutions and periods of calm. To understand, for example, the contemporary history of Eastern Europe, one must look closely at the years between 1945 and 1948, when the system that has lasted forty years was put into place. Textbooks on history, by the nature of things, tend to deal in cursory fashion with decisive periods because they must cover long stretches of time. They cannot afford to spend too much time on details, such as a leadership contest or an election result, that might later turn out to be extremely important.

For this reason, it is difficult to reconstitute in a textbook the climate or feelings of a given period. Yet isn't this the most interesting aspect? The past, which interests us and whose outcome we know, was once the present, full of uncertainties and possibilities, with its calculations and miscalculations, with doors that opened and blocked off other doors that might otherwise have been unlocked.

Open Mandates

Jean Marchand, in 1968, was Lester Pearson's first choice as leader of the Liberal Party of Canada. For his own reasons, Marchand deferred to Pierre Trudeau, who was an unwilling candidate. In the end, Michael Pitfield and Marc Lalonde managed to persuade him. The rest is history: his election at the head of the party on the fourth ballot, April 6, 1968, and the subsequent general election in which Trudeaumania played a leading role.

At this point, there are two key considerations. First, had Marchand or an anglophone been chosen by the Liberal convention, Canadian history would have taken a different course. Marchand was closer to Quebec than was Trudeau and less doctrinaire about constitutional and linguistic issues. An anglophone would naturally have followed a different road than the one taken by Trudeau. Secondly, Trudeau did not produce a specific government program during the leadership race or in the course of the election campaign.[1] "New guys with new ideas" was the rallying cry during the leadership campaign. With Trudeau, Canada was going to enter the future: the cybernetic revolution, no less.

Had English Canada realized the extent to which Trudeau's ideas on language were new and radical, Trudeaumania would never have gotten off the ground. Indeed, the party might never have elected Trudeau to lead it, not because it was hostile to this linguistic revolution but because it would never have thought it marketable in English Canada.

Let us be clear about one thing. The democratic process confers legitimacy, except in cases of actual misrepresentation. If a party manages to be elected without promising anything, without committing itself to anything, its legitimacy is intact. Voters make a choice and live with the consequences. A party is elected to govern, and no one can anticipate the problems that will crop up in the course of its mandate. Obviously, some commitments are more serious than others, and there is some risk in ignoring them. If voters believe that their confidence was misplaced, they will act accordingly next time. These are the rules of the game.

Interpreting the voters' mandate is part of the game of politics. It assumes greater importance in our parliamentary system, which gives considerable authority to the prime minister. There are few countervailing powers. There are no institutional means of imposing a referendum on the government, which enjoys sweeping powers by virtue of the constitution. Moreover, the prime minister has the exclusive prerogative of appointments for politically meaningful posts and for judges of the Supreme Court, who will be the ultimate arbiters of the Constitution.

In other words, our system of government favours the politics of the *fait accompli*. A prime minister may have more than four years ahead of him to smooth out an initially hostile reaction to a reform, which in any event will be only one issue among many by the time the next election comes round. So it was that bilingualism was not a major issue in the election of October 1972, even though it was the first one after the introduction of this new policy. Another example is that of wage and price controls, imposed in the fall of 1975 and ending in 1978, which played a marginal role in the election of May 1979.

But the policy of bilingualism had an additional advantage.

Ethnic Power

The leeway enjoyed by the prime minister is all the greater in a multinational federation where ethnic reflexes weigh heavily on the vote. At the outset, Pierre Trudeau could count on 25 percent of the seats in Parliament. To form a government, he needed to win only a quarter of the ridings in English Canada; he needed only 35 percent for a majority. He could therefore put up with the enmity of an entire region, which was his attitude concerning the four western provinces with one quarter of the Canadian population.

What is the meaning of the ethnic vote? For Pierre Trudeau, who benefited from it more than anyone else, all it amounts to is a tribal reflex. For a sociologist, it comes from a natural solidarity combined with self-interest. But no matter what the term is, the result is the same: extreme indulgence towards a native son who excels on a large rink. *As long as Pierre Trudeau did not visibly harm Quebec, he could count on its votes.*

Because he advanced the cause of French-Canadians in Ottawa and disturbed a number of anglophones with a certain flair, the rest of his program — the ode to the Canadian nation — hardly mattered. The proof came late in the day, during the referendum campaign in Quebec, when a large number of people were convinced that Pierre Trudeau had changed and that he had taken a major step in *their* direction. Had they really listened to Trudeau during all these years, they would have known that it was all done with mirrors.

Thus the man who was prime minister of Canada for sixteen years enjoyed considerable leeway with voters in Quebec. This was the source of the great misunderstanding. Trudeau was able to confound the opponents of his language policy by invoking the strong electoral mandates he received from Quebec: *his* vision of Canada projected that of Quebec's voters, and Canada had to accept that if it wanted to survive. This sorcerer's dialectic, very effective for a time, not only served the cause of bilingualism but also facilitated the constitutional isolation of Quebec in November 1981. English Canada's abysmal ignorance of Quebec was also a strong factor.

Indeed, even after voters in Quebec triumphantly returned Brian Mulroney, whose conception of Canada differed radically from that of Pierre Trudeau, English Canada continued to take Trudeau more seriously. Canadians thus underestimate the effect on Quebec of the failure of Meech, a failure for which Trudeau is primarily responsible. (Unfortunately, we will never know who would have carried Quebec in the federal election of September 1984 had Trudeau not resigned. The outcome would have been hard to predict.)

The great misunderstanding has thus persisted right to the end.

The misunderstanding was perpetuated not only by anglophones who reluctantly followed Trudeau but also by those who opposed him. Neither group questioned the role he assumed of spokesman for Quebec. It was a case of mistaken identity: opponents believed that by rejecting him they were rejecting Quebec's view of Canada. The debate was booby-trapped from the start. Twenty years were lost by neglecting certain doors concealed in the shadows and now locked for good as a result of the inevitable backlash.

The Secrets of the Ballot Box

From the very moment he entered politics, Trudeau used the argument of electoral victory for his own purposes. Let us have a close look at these victories. English Canada, which practically coincides with the nine provinces other than Quebec,* gave him a majority of seats in 1968 but with only a plurality of the votes. It was the first and last time. In 1968, he had not submitted any precise program to the voters. When English Canada had the opportunity of passing judgement on his government, and this happened four times, they never gave him a majority of seats. They persistently gave the Conservatives a larger number of seats. The disproportion was particularly humiliating in 1972 and 1979. These events were lost in the general Canadian results. Yet never at any time has English Canada ratified Trudeau's vision of Canada.

Since no election has ever been a referendum on coast-

* Numerically, Montreal ridings with anglophone majorities are approximately equivalent to francophone ridings in New Brunswick, Ontario, and Manitoba.

Federal Election Results, 1968–1980, in Seats

	1968 EC	1968 FC	1972 EC	1972 FC	1974 EC	1974 FC	1979 EC	1979 FC	1980 EC	1980 FC
Liberals	99	56	54	56	81	60	47	67	73	74
Conservatives	69	4	105	2	92	3	134	2	102	1
NDP	22	0	31	0	16	0	26	0	32	0
Socred	0	14	0	15	0	11	0	6	0	0
Total	190	74	190	74	190	74	207	75	207	75

EC: English Canada; FC: French Canada.
Sources: *Canada Yearbook*, different years

to-coast bilingualism, one cannot say that it was formally rejected by English Canada. Nevertheless, the attitude of the Conservative Party on this question was ambiguous until the advent of Brian Mulroney in 1983. Election results show that the issue never had enthusiastic support in English Canada, to say the least.

Canadian opinion can be examined from another angle. We know that Quebec clearly expressed its linguistic vision of Canada in provincial elections. Similarly, from 1968 until the end of the eighties, no anglophone province, with the exception of New Brunswick, did anything for linguistic equality on its own territory. Two provinces, Saskatchewan and Alberta, even took a step backward from legal equality. (At the end of the eighties, Ontario acted positively on the matter of French services in areas where justified by numbers, a move that reinforced the current backlash against bilingualism.) English-Canadian opinion on the question is therefore quite clear.

It is true that the constitution of 1982 established linguistic equality in education. Minorities may benefit from it wherever justified by numbers. The concession was wrested from the provincial premiers at the very end of the constitutional conference of November 1981. But this demographic restriction creates innumerable problems — and the steady stream of petitioners before the courts are being supported financially by the federal treasury.[2] Real progress is therefore minimal. It is important to note also that this constitution was never ratified by universal suffrage.

It is an amazing paradox. Quebec did not subscribe to Pierre Trudeau's Canadian vision, and neither did English Canada, yet that vision ruled the land for sixteen years — and even longer, since Brian Mulroney took it over with a more cautious packaging. Some misunderstandings can be very expensive. This one would eventually turn against its originator: an idea endlessly repeated eventually makes an impression. The alternative "coast-to-coast bilingualism or the breakup of Canada" was finally imprinted in the minds on both sides of the language barrier, particularly among Quebec federalists. The actual process leading to bilingualism is necessarily interpreted differently by each language community: minorities that have historically deplored its absence show their impatience while majorities tend to make haste slowly. Accordingly, in the end, political sentiment was bound to converge in a questioning of the very basis of the country's existence.

The constant affirmation of Quebec's French character could only help reinforce such a meeting of minds. When the Liberal government of Quebec upheld Bill 101, notwithstanding an unfavourable decision of the Supreme Court of Canada, English Canada could only conclude that it had been suckered into a bad deal: "These Quebecers want a bilingual Canada everywhere...save in Quebec. Enough is enough." Even though majorities have a lazy conscience, it is still surprising that so many Canadians readily accepted the prospect of Canada's breakup, without wondering if there wasn't a better conceptual framework for defining Canada than Pierre Trudeau's.

Dual Legitimacy

A permanent electoral misunderstanding is characteristic of all heterogeneous federations and raises the problem of dual legitimacy. Who is the ultimate spokesperson for a region or a province? The premier of that province, members of the House of Commons elected from that province, or the prime minister of the country? In 1978, faced with mounting demands from the provinces, Pierre Trudeau cried out: "But who will speak for Canada?" If the problem exists for the whole of Canada, one can easily imagine how acute it must be in Quebec, where 90 percent of all French-Canadians are concentrated, and where the government is jealous of its constitutional prerogatives.

Many political analysts in Quebec and Canada have developed a theory explaining the electoral behaviour of Quebec voters: their strategy is to avoid putting all their eggs in one basket. When voting provincially they take into account whatever is happening on the federal scene, and one presumes that the converse is also true. "Red in Ottawa, blue in Quebec" is therefore the result of a historical reflex that Quebec voters are able to manipulate to their advantage.

It is an attractive theory, one that flatters voters in Quebec for being extraordinarily cunning in their approach to Canadian politics. This is precisely the reason why it is so widely invoked. But does it really explain anything?

Even superficially, Quebec's history offers no confirmation. Since Confederation, the periods when the same party was in power in Quebec and in Ottawa have been far longer than when the opposite was true. The situation has occurred twice since the end of World War II, during two crucial periods in the history of Quebec, 1963 to 1966 and 1970 to 1976. In fact, if it hadn't been for the rather accidental election of Daniel Johnson in 1966, because of the electoral system and the presence of a third party, the RIN (Rassemblement pour l'indépendance nationale), there would have been a continuous Red or Liberal period from

1963 to 1976. Since 1984, parties sharing more or less the same outlook have ruled in Quebec and Ottawa.

Reality leaves the theory behind in a more fundamental way still. For each election, voters feel compelled to choose between two main parties *because of the voting system.* The number of options is necessarily limited. People vote on the basis of a number of proposals put forward by competing parties, and these are not really applicable to another political realm. Symmetry or asymmetry is dictated by circumstances more than anything else.

It would be extravagant to say that Jean Lesage was elected solely as a counterweight to John Diefenbaker, or René Lévesque to Pierre Trudeau. Robert Bourassa opposed Trudeau in 1971 in Victoria, in 1974 at the time of Bill 22, and in 1976 on the question of funding the Olympic Games in Montreal. The truth of the matter is that, since 1944, *all* governments in Quebec have clashed with Ottawa.

It would be just as extravagant to say that Lester Pearson and Pierre Trudeau were elected to "protect" Quebecers from the government of Quebec. In fact, the federal Liberal Party enjoyed a near monopoly of the Quebec vote, this for historical reasons going back to the conscription crisis of 1917. The only exception was the election of John Diefenbaker in 1958. In the two main federal parties, Quebec voters felt less like strangers with the federal Liberals.

The alternation of parties in power in Quebec had little to do with the same phenomenon at the federal level. During the years of the Parti Québécois, from the end of 1976 to the end of 1985, Trudeau managed to broaden his support in Quebec until February 1980, when he almost wiped out the opposition, taking 74 of the 75 seats. Were voters inspired by a desire for balance?

With 70 percent of the vote, Trudeau must have had substantial support from *souverainistes* (lukewarm perhaps, but certainly not federalists in the Trudeau mould!). The explanation for this unique performance lies in the parallel decline of the Créditistes' share of the vote, which the provincial election of November 1976 had already illustrated. Given the anachronistic and marginal character of their party, Créditiste voters had nowhere to turn but to Trudeau.

One of the rare constants in Canadian politics since 1945 is that Quebec voters, having to choose between a native leader and a non-native one, have always favoured the native. It may be strategic to vote as a bloc, but it has little to do with balancing Quebec against Ottawa. And this leads right into the deadlock of dual legitimacy.

The Boomerang

The year 1980 was an exceptional one for federal Liberals in Quebec. They swept everything before them: the federal election in February and then the referendum in May. They walked on water. Their faces were radiant with the elixir of power. If they didn't have a mandate, who else could claim to have one?

What followed deserves analysis and comment. But first, let us consider for a moment how History rests on petty details and grand ironies.

In the election of May 1979, the Liberals were truly trounced in English Canada, where they won only 47 of 207 seats. But in Quebec they gained 7 seats, of which five were formerly Créditiste, for a total of 67. Joe Clark formed a minority government, 6 seats short of a majority. As it happened, the Créditistes had salvaged 6 seats and, for the first time in a long while, they were in a position to exert a certain influence on national policy.

Subsequent events are well known. In November 1979, Trudeau announced his departure from political life. In December, the Conservative government tabled an austerity budget, which included a new tax of 18 cents on a gallon of gasoline. A group of Liberals concocted a scheme to trip the government when the budget came up for a vote, which would automatically bring about a new election...and possibly the return of Pierre Trudeau, who was then only interim leader.

What followed was tragicomical. The Créditistes, who took their cue directly from the Premier's Office in Quebec City, received no guidance about this "trivial" vote.[3] In doubt, they abstained. Their decision helped bring down the Conservative government, ensuring the return of Pierre Trudeau. His victory in 1980 was a veritable triumph in Quebec, which provided half of the total Liberal contingent in Ottawa. Another consequence of the Créditiste decision was that they themselves were wiped out. The race was a tight one in English Canada, hence every seat counted. The Liberal machine therefore made every effort in the eight non-Liberal ridings in Quebec, where only Roch Lasalle managed to survive, and barely. Six fewer seats and the Liberals would have been forced into a minority government.

The same Quebec voters who ensured Pierre Trudeau's political survival in May 1979 and gave him a landslide victory in 1980 were surprised a few months later to see the steamroller of unilateral constitutional patriation coming in their direction. The great misunderstanding would spring like a mousetrap on Quebec.

CHAPTER 4

The Scrambled Eggs of Canadian Federalism

Here we are, then, at the beginning of the eighties, at the heart of the Canadian problem. Suppose that some understanding was possible between Quebec and English Canada on the linguistic definition of the country. It is not an unreasonable proposition. After all, Robert Stanfield and Joe Clark, who each led the Conservative Party from 1967 to 1983, accepted the broad outline of the "two nations" concept. It cannot be repeated too often that it was Quebecers who blocked this crucial idea west of the Ottawa River.

However, even if the question could have been resolved conclusively, Canada would still be in trouble. Another contentious issue would still hang over our heads: the division of powers, the second axis in our little constitutional chart on page 10. It has been in the forefront since 1945.

Earlier, to finance the war effort, the federal government had "rented" taxation powers from the provinces in return for annual payments. It solemnly promised to abandon them once the war was over. However, by the end of this horrible carnage and after almost six years of economic and social mobilization, things had changed considerably.

With the demobilization of the armed forces and of the civilians directly involved in war production, there loomed the old spectres of mass unemployment and depression. Only the war had really curbed them. No economist anticipated the incredible postwar surprise of prosperity. All were agreed on one point: the absolute necessity of state intervention to prevent the recurrence of the Great Depression. In 1945–46, economic laissez-faire was totally discredited. Great Britain was already laying the foundations of the welfare state, and the "heretical" ideas of John Maynard Keynes were being enthusiastically received throughout the English-speaking world.

The Canadian government had developed some muscle as a result of its management of the war effort. A new bureaucracy had emerged. Inexperienced provincial governments were felt to be in no position to secure economic stability and social progress. Accordingly, taxes stayed where they were in 1945: in Ottawa.

A Flexible Constitution

There was a little snag. By virtue of the British North America Act of 1867, social policy was exclusively within provincial jurisdiction. However, Ottawa had two ways of getting around the problem. The first was to persuade the provinces to relinquish certain powers in Ottawa's favour, as had been the case with unemployment insurance at the beginning of World War II. This was repeated in 1951 with old age pensions. The federal government had the money and the provinces did not want to deprive elderly people of federal benefits or subject them to double taxation, against which voters would have rebelled.

The second solution, simpler because it did not require a constitutional amendment, had to do with the federal government's constitutional *right to spend* for the general welfare of the country. Ottawa could transfer funds to the provinces for specific programs, which they administered themselves. Ottawa set standards while funding was jointly provided, thereby preserving constitutional proprieties. A province rejecting this intrusion — and Premier Maurice Duplessis did it for postsecondary education — was, of course, cutting itself off from federal largesse. (In this instance, the sums due to Quebec were recovered after the death of Duplessis.)

These were the so-called joint programs (health care and welfare being the best known), which caused so much friction between Quebec and Ottawa in the days of Jean Lesage.[1] The premier wanted Quebec to have the right to withdraw from those programs infringing on provincial jurisdiction, with matching compensation in the form of income tax points. An agreement was signed in 1964 providing for provincial opting out with fiscal compensation and maintenance of national standards during a transition period.

Daniel Johnson went further, demanding the end of joint programs and a new division of powers, more advantageous for Quebec, particularly in social and cultural policy, which would be at the heart of a brand-new constitution.

Politicians come and go...but constitutional conferences remain. Early in 1980, little had changed from 1968. Joint programs were still in force along with their national standards.

Meanwhile, a new idea was making headway: that Confederation was threatened with balkanization as a result of expanding provincial powers and the premiers' tendency to behave like petty barons. In the realm of hand-me-down ideas, this one makes it to the top of the list.

The Postage Stamp Complex

What were these notions based on? On the fact that the provinces controlled an ever larger part of Canada's tax resources. In 1950, for instance, federal revenues were two and a half times the sum of provincial revenues. Twenty years later, they were almost equal, and, by 1988, the provinces were ahead by close to 14 percent.[2] This inversion in the growth rate of tax revenues took place between 1960 and 1984. Since 1985, Ottawa's budget problems have required a steep rise in tax collections, with the result that its revenues are now rising faster than those of the provinces.

There is more. More than one-fifth of all federal revenues are paid out to the provinces in the form of transfer payments for equalization purposes and federal participation in joint programs. Figures for the 1986–87 fiscal year (the last available for our analysis) show that these payments constitute 23 percent of the Quebec government's total revenues. They must be added to the province's own revenues. When these transfer payments are considered in relation to the total amount Quebec taxpayers pay to Ottawa,[3] one can infer that Quebec "controls" 65 percent of the taxes paid by its residents, compared with Ottawa's 35 percent. How can one ask for more?

This is the essence of the transfer payments argument.

Some analysts will include in their calculations the revenues of local institutions such as municipalities, hospitals, and school boards. This further reduces the importance of the federal government. As yet, no one seems to have included all the voluntary "taxes" that consumers pay for food, clothing, shelter, and recreation. This is unfortunate, because it would really begin to sink in that the role of the federal government has shrunk to the size of a postage stamp.

There are many avenues of investigation for those who want a clear and unprejudiced view. But one must differentiate between control of tax revenues and the balance sheet of federalism. Quebec might control only 40 percent of tax revenues without federalism being profitable, or it could receive 80 percent of tax revenues and still win out on its federal ties. However, what we are discussing here is that intangible reality called *power*.

Changes in Federal and Provincial Revenues in Canada
(in millions of current dollars)

	Federal Revenues	Federal Transfers To Other Levels of Government	Provincial Revenues	Provincial Transfers To Local Governments
1950	3,020	251	1,226	171
1960	6,517	994	3,319	714
1970	15,538	3,397	13,890	5,394
1980	50,653	12,831	59,254	19,512
1988	110,122	24,706	125,026	37,450

Source: Department of Finance, Canada, *Annual Reference Tables*, June 1989.
N.B.: These are current dollars. Inflation was generally low from 1950 to 1970. Provincial revenues include federal transfers.

Will the Real Power Raise Its Hand?

Behind these fiscal statistics are certain realities ignored by federal mandarins and the media who relay their ideas. First of all, in what way does control of tax revenues determine trends in the relative power of governments?

Let us, for example, look at municipalities. The increasingly rapid urbanization of industrial societies since 1945 has brought about an explosive growth in local expenditures on urban infrastructure, mass transit, and police. Accordingly, property taxes have become more important. Ottawa has no constitutional authority in these matters. But how does the growing importance of local government affect the relative strength of Ottawa? Does it impinge on its fields of jurisdiction? Does it weaken its ability to provide leadership on national issues? Not in the least.

In reality, the federal government has far more initiative in municipal affairs than municipalities in federal affairs. Municipalities are always begging for federal funds, while Ottawa very seldom begs from municipalities. At the proper moment, Ottawa will set out its conditions. The crowning touch is that Ottawa is not obliged to pay property taxes.

So much for municipalities. Let us examine other local authorities: hospitals and school boards. It will allow us to put the finger on the curious lack of symmetry residing in the argument of transfer payments.

Yes, there are significant federal budget transfers to the provinces. However, one forgets that these allocations represent sums that, from a balance-sheet perspective, are merely conveyed through provincial governments to school and hospital authorities. As a whole, the provinces pay in transfer payments to local administrations *one and a half times what they receive* from the federal government. In 1988, it came to $37.5 billion paid out versus $24.7 billion received. Therefore, if transfer payments adversely affect the relative power of the federal government, they must have an even greater impact on the provinces.

Let us pursue this question further. There is an essential qualitative difference between federal and provincial transfers. The flow of federal funds can be slowed down, and for certain joint programs even cut off completely, not immediately, but over a few years. It is true, the principle of equalization was written into the Canadian constitution in 1982, but the method by which they are calculated is wholly discretionary. Indeed, in 1982, Ottawa reduced payments by revamping the law on Fiscal Arrangements.

There are no legislative guarantees at all for funding established programs, the official way of referring to budget allocations to the provinces for health care and postsecondary education. Ottawa may increase or cut back its contributions according to circumstances. The federal budget of February 1990 introduced cutbacks for the third time in five years.[4]

The parameters of the Canada Assistance Plan for the "have" provinces were also modified for the first time by the same budget. Ottawa used to assume 50 percent of provincial expenditures on welfare, but no longer. So the 50 percent rule is not immutable. Planners in the "have-not" provinces must be asking themselves some hard questions.

How does a province react to these successive shocks? It is here that the difference between the two levels of government becomes clear. A province has no means of fiscal retaliation against the federal government. It might think of urging its people to mount the barricades, but this is not the way things are done here — and there is no guarantee that it would work. In Ottawa's case, a simple law or budget can do the trick. A provincial government has no recourse but to raise taxes or cut real expenditures. Since education and health care take up half of Quebec's revenues, they are bound to be affected by any kind of cutback.

These are sensitive sectors. Furthermore, schools and hospitals are *independent.* They are not run by the government. They have every possibility of informing the population of the hardships they face. The war of nerves has been going on for ten years. There must be days when provincial authorities would like to hand over the whole mess to Ottawa!

And this is what takes the cake. Federal cash payments cover 16 percent of provincial expenditures on health care in Quebec. But the money is paid only if certain conditions are met, and these requirements are not trifling. Ottawa demands that Medicare be nothing less than comprehensive, universal, transferable, and free of charge.[5] In 1984, it brought in legislation that put an end to extra billing by doctors in certain provinces of English Canada.

It is obvious that an aging population is going to be a heavy drag on Medicare. But the point here is not to criticize or endorse the conditions imposed by Ottawa. It is simply to point out that, with a mere contribution of $1.5 billion, Ottawa is able to set the parameters of a system on which another government is spending $7.5 billion. If this is not *real* power, what is?

Some people will say it is normal for the piper to call the tune. At one time, expenditures were shared fifty-fifty, and, had this not been a purely provincial field of jurisdiction, it would have been perfectly normal. So there are two reasons for believing such a mode of operation is not normal. But let us put them aside for just a moment.

Looking at this situation, a foreign observer might be moved to say: "Here is a very fussy government, but with its heart if not its wallet in the right place. And whenever it is transferring money from the have to the have-not provinces, one of its essential functions, it surely sees to it that all is well spent."

Indeed, Ottawa has the power but makes no use of it.

Our foreign observer would stare in disbelief if told that equalization grants from Ottawa to have-not provinces have absolutely *no strings attached* to ensure that public services are in fact comparable in quality to those of the wealthier provinces. No questions asked. No audits for the $6 billion paid out for 1989–90. The observer would only have to read the pertinent text from the Department of Finance: "The federal government does not impose on the provinces levels of public services or taxation rates. The provinces are free to decide on these matters. Equalization payments are thus unconditional. Provinces are free to use them as they choose."[6]

What seems normal in one case is not in the other.

Welcome to the rational federalism of Pierre Elliott Trudeau.

Wall-to-Wall Federalism

Casting a line in the murky waters of Canadian fiscal policy, one pulls out a funny fish with a very large head. All important transfer programs addressed to individuals are still within federal jurisdiction: old age pensions, unemployment insurance, and family allowances. Each province may devise its own programs, which, obviously, cannot be as generous. Anything affecting more than one province is also an exclusive federal responsibility: for instance, transportation, communications, money and banking, interprovincial trade. Individual firms in these fields are subject only to federal regulation. Anything concerning international relations (national defense, foreign trade, and foreign relations) comes under federal authority.

One can see that money is not the only source of power. The right of intervention and *regulation* is another very important one. The best example is monetary policy. Materially, its administration costs next to nothing, but it has a direct effect on every Canadian, landlords or tenants, savers or borrowers, executives or wage-earners. Everyone knows in concrete terms what rising or falling interest rates mean.

Not a single provincial expenditure of similar size has a comparable impact. And one knows how jealously Ottawa will defend its prerogatives in this particular field.

The British North America Act of 1867 created two levels of government and gave each exclusive authority over specific areas. The general idea was that matters of local interest would be provincial and matters of national importance would be federal. There were two areas of concurrent jurisdiction, agriculture and immigration, but with priority given to the federal government. Anything not specifically attributed to the provinces was within federal jurisdiction.

Today, it would be difficult to name more than a few general areas (primary and secondary education being the most important) not directly or indirectly under the influence of federal policy through subsidies or regulation. During the last fifty years or so, the private garden of the provinces has become just a little plot for members of the family. In other words, overlapping jurisdictions are the norm rather than the exception. The best way to understand this is to look beyond individual programs, taking a sectoral perspective.

It is not our purpose here to claim that the provinces have little freedom. On the contrary, Quebec has large independent revenues and has all the latitude it needs in a variety of programs. Nor are we interested in determining which level of government does a better job, even if it were possible to answer such a question. There are good programs and muddled programs in Ottawa as in Quebec.

Again, our purpose is to look at respective powers and the *internal consistency* of the system at the present time. It is necessary to dwell a little on this point to understand the general principle at the root of the numerous issues opposing Quebec and Ottawa on the division of powers.

Some examples among others will be mentioned here. The Quebec Pension Plan is solely within provincial jurisdiction, while old age pensions are paid out by the federal government. In these circumstances, how does one determine an *integrated* policy for senior citizens? Unemployment insurance is federal, while welfare is provincial. Education is provincial, while vocational training is a joint jurisdiction. How, then, can one design a *single* policy for the workplace?

Over the last few years, family policy has taken very opposite directions in Ottawa and Quebec. Taxation policy in Quebec must take federal fiscal policy into account, although the reverse is seldom true. And so on. Not mentioned here are areas where the two levels of government act independently, such as culture and scientific research.

In the beginning, all these areas were attributed to the provinces. In exchange, is there any area of federal jurisdiction that the provinces have entered in a definitive way? None. Of course, this would not have improved the consistency of the system. However, in all sectors where there is overlapping authority, either the priorities of the two levels of government are identical, making one of them superfluous, or else they diverge, with the consequent problems of economic *and* political inefficiency and accountability.

Those who claim that Canadian federalism is excessively decentralized are right in saying that the federal government's leeway has been seriously eroded during the last few years. This is because budget policy has been among the most lax in the Western world from 1978 to 1985 and has brought on the present deficit crisis. Meanwhile, certain provinces, including Quebec, have had a very rough time and have had to use an axe rather than a scalpel to keep expenditures in check. And this is the proof of the undoubted pre-eminence of the federal government: no province could have accumulated such large deficits (relative to its tax base) without being restrained by money markets.

Eventually, however, the red ink can no longer dry and the lid must be replaced on the inkwell. In the weeping capital, mandarins are shedding tears over spilt ink. Wall-to-wall federalism is not easy.

Quebec Resistance

Every government in Quebec since 1960 has rebelled against this constant overlapping of jurisdictions. All the constitutional projects developed in Quebec since 1965 have aimed, as a minimum, at restoring the spirit prevailing at Confederation in 1867: federal withdrawal from the areas of provincial jurisdiction occupied over the years and a *clear* division of powers between the two levels of government. As the federal government withdrew, it would grant Quebec the necessary fiscal means to exercise its old "new" powers. Daniel Johnson considered this was just the beginning and that the British North America Act should be redrawn from scratch. The new division of powers would allow Quebec to exercise its role as "the national State of French Canadians." Even Robert Bourassa claimed "cultural sovereignty," in other words, all the powers relating to culture.[7]

The mail clerk on duty at the Langevin Block in Ottawa, where the Prime Minister's Office is located, might as well have returned all constitutional documents from Quebec to the sender. The gulf between Quebec and Ottawa was unbridgeable, and not only because of Pierre Trudeau's rigidity. No government will give up its authority unless it is forced to do so. Trudeau shocked a large number of people on questions of form, but he was basically in line with contemporary developments in Canada.

It is important to recall the circumstances in which the Quebec Pension Plan was established in 1964. Ottawa had decided to go ahead with its own Canada Pension Plan, whose apparent advantage was to ease labour mobility from province to province without jeopardizing accumulated pension benefits. What was a provincial area of jurisdiction was dressed up to look like a federal one.

Quebec pushed ahead with its own pension scheme, well thought out and very different with respect to the use of accumulated funds. The federal plan invests solely in provincial bonds, while the Caisse de dépôt in Quebec has a much broader portfolio. Ottawa finally accepted the Quebec plan, and benefits are transferable from one fund to the other.

Quebec had to fight to retain control of a jurisdiction that had been exclusively its own! And Quebec thought that Ottawa was willing to give up joint programs and send compensatory tax points all nicely wrapped up? The federal government never honoured the promise made more or less explicitly by Lester Pearson in 1964, when the provinces were allowed to withdraw from existing joint programs.[8] As for the rest...

Right from the beginning, there was a misunderstanding on the very meaning of words. When Quebec spoke of the constitution, it meant the British North America Act of 1867. For Ottawa the constitution included all that had evolved since 1867. In other words, it meant contemporary practice: that interpretation was flexible enough to allow Ottawa to play its national role. Legally everything was in order, although the constitution could be amended only by an act of the British Parliament because, when the country formally became independent in 1931, Canadians could not agree on an amending formula. One day, the old parchment would have to be repatriated, but meanwhile it worked very well. There had been in fact quite a few amendments. But, because the provinces had a sort of veto on repatriation, they kept raising the ante. They were being unreasonable.

Quebec was in effect using its veto to link repatriation with a new division of powers. Jean Lesage was repudiated by public opinion for having failed to do so during discussions on the Fulton-Favreau formula of 1964. (Who nowadays remembers that Pierre Trudeau objected to the formula for not giving sufficient protection to Quebec's present powers?)[9]

This strategic linkage, however, could only lead up a constitutional blind alley, whence the failure of the Fulton-Favreau formula, the setbacks suffered by Daniel Johnson and Jean-Jacques Bertrand, and that suffered by Robert Bourassa in Victoria in 1971, when Pierre Trudeau refused to recognize Quebec's pre-eminence in social policy.

During all those years, Quebec was unable to prevent federal raids by Ottawa on its own constitutional territory. The federal system was no less a hybrid in 1980 than in 1965 — and Quebec had failed to recover a single power, except through administrative agreements with the federal government, notably concerning family allowances and immigration. But these agreements contain no solid guarantees as to their duration. Ottawa likes it that way. Let us anticipate the events that would jolt the 1980s: the Meech Lake Accord brings only a slight corrective to this hybrid character.

An Outmoded Perfume

This background makes it easier to appreciate at its true worth a type of argument widely used from 1960 to about 1980, and which was the federalist answer to the rise of the sovereigntist arguments. The argument retains a certain charm today, removed as it is from the real movement of history, like those old magazines that remind us of bygone days full of unkept promises.

These writings and speeches claimed that federalism was the *best* possible form of government, a higher stage of human evolution. First, it offered a guarantee of liberty, since power was shared and balanced. It also had a functional division of power, local matters being in the hands of the provinces and national affairs in federal hands. Finally, it stood in the mainstream of history: after a long period of nationalist excesses, Europe was ready for supranationality.

With the rise of separatism, the people of *Cité libre* became very fond of this type of talk. And then they came to power...and ignored many of their previous pronouncements. Twenty-five years later, it should be evident that this discourse has not successfully passed the test of time.

Canadian federalism has little to do with the nice theoretical constructs of an intellectual coterie. Eggs, cream, and butter under federal management, fresh milk, chicken and pork in the hands of the provinces, professional training for employees of small businesses administered by the provinces and for employees of large enterprises by the federal government, immigration and the environment split between both levels — one needs a very special set of rose-coloured glasses to see here any indication of rational organization. And all this is accompanied by an exorbitant federal spending power, which Trudeau himself condemned in 1961.[10]

Are the nation-states of old Europe closer to a true European federation than they were in 1960? Not at all, as we will see in Chapter 8. Does liberty flourish more in Western federal countries than in Western unitary states? No. There are countries where geography, history, or ethnic diversity impose a federal constitution, and some people have made a religion out of this necessity. But nowhere in the West is there a small homogeneous country that has chosen federalism as a mode of government. Which brings us to the central question at the heart of relations between Quebec and Canada.

The One True Question

The question has been hanging for twenty-five years. It has nothing to do with francophones succeeding in Ottawa (the answer is obvious), nor with Quebec's performance compared with Ottawa (it depends on policy areas). It asks why is it advantageous for Quebec, a small society of 6.8 million people, to continue spreading its talents and resources so thinly between two conflicting levels of government?

When one hears that federalism has been the better option for Quebec, the instinctive interpretation is "better than independence." However, independence did not emerge as a plausible alternative until the 1960s. Yet, in 1867, there was another option, which Quebec never considered seriously, and that was *legislative union.* It was because of Quebec that Canada took the road of federalism. But Canada East, as Quebec was then called, could have accepted union subject to receiving the same language and educational guarantees as under the federal solution.

Knowing how things have turned out since then, it is difficult to imagine how legislative union could have been worse for Quebec than federalism as we have known it. On the contrary, it might have been beneficial in many respects, as shown indirectly by the experience with the Union government between 1841 and 1867,[11] which definitely laid to rest Durham's goal of assimilation and encouraged the rise of a solid French-Canadian political class. French-Canadians would have enjoyed a higher profile in the public service of Canada, and the Catholic Church would not have exercised the same degree of control on Quebec society. At the time, Quebec had about one-third of the Canadian population established on a narrow band of territory. The Quebec group in Ottawa would have assumed the heavy responsibility of promoting French-Canadian interests. It would have been a truly "*beau risque.*"*

Would economic and social maturity have come more quickly to Quebec under these circumstances? Considering the chain of events that began in 1920 in the cultural field, with the beginning of radio, it is difficult to answer this

*After Brian Mulroney's victory in September 1984, René Lévesque suggested that a new federalism might be possible, and it was worth the risk of trying it out. Federalism had become "a *beau risque.*"

question negatively. An inventory of cultural initiatives by the two levels of government leaves little doubt on this score. The federal government has done infinitely more for the cultural advancement of French Canada than has the provincial government. Just consider Radio-Canada. Also consider that, under a legislative union, it would have been far more difficult to close down French schools outside Quebec.

And to think that conventional wisdom assigns education and culture to the provinces!

With the passage of time, however, the relative importance of Quebec would have declined, making the clashes between majority and minority far more intense than what we have already experienced. The rejection of Quebec would have assumed serious proportions, as in 1990! The idea of independence or of decentralized federalism would have taken shape. To anyone recommending federalism as now practised as a possible solution, the reply would have been: "What you are proposing is a hybrid system that solves none of the problems connected with legislative union. The rule of the majority over the minority is preserved in too many sectors. We should keep in common only what needs to be."

In 1867, federalism was the easy way out for Quebec, and the province fell into the trap. Today, legislative union is not a realistic option because Quebec's demographic importance is constantly declining. Furthermore, the attachment of Quebecers to their homeland-province and of English Canadians to their diverse regions would constitute an insurmountable obstacle.

Even the appearance in Ottawa of a strong central government on the American model is not plausible. It must be pointed out, however, that the Canadian prime minister has far more authority than the American president, and that the promotion of regional interests is assumed in the United States by the two houses of Congress, whose members are not subject to party discipline.[12]

So what choice is left for Quebec? The eighties have placed this question under a cold spotlight.

CHAPTER 5

Sunny May, Rainy November

Although it took a long time, René Lévesque and Pierre Trudeau were finally face to face in the ring. Most people have forgotten that the fight was almost cancelled for lack of interest. Lévesque won the first round handily with Bill 101. And then, in 1978–79, the round of constitutional talks failed miserably, in spite of many concessions on Trudeau's part. Even though a constitution might be called the most important document in a democracy, the discussions preceding the birth are more often than not conducted with forceps. Trudeau knew his days were numbered, while the provinces feigned interest, waiting for Joe Clark. And the referee, the Canadian people, fired the first and installed the second — on a rickety chair.

Joe Clark came, he saw, and he tripped. Pierre Trudeau came back, he saw, and he conquered. It took him only twenty-one months to demolish the premier of Quebec completely.

The Quebec Fudge

Successive governments in Quebec took refuge behind their veto to demand sweeping changes in the division of powers. Pierre Trudeau had great fun ridiculing these quests for a status that was more or less special. The demands were just an intellectual game and they contained a flaw that would turn out to be fatal. These exercises rested on an Olympian conception of political life: people of goodwill are having an elegant discussion around a table; to be heard, they must remain calm and state their legitimate claims; at the end of the day, the most cogent and articulate position wins out.

Perhaps there is a remote planet where the universe unfolds according to this scenario, but among humans things are different. What is the relative strength of the parties present? What groups can be aroused to defend a set of propositions? And, above all, how can a refusal, even a courteous one, be answered? Not a single constitutional document gathering dust on an obscure library shelf answers any of these questions. "Between people of goodwill, it is always possible to agree" and "right is on our side" have been the dominant themes of almost thirty years of constitutional babbling in Quebec.

Meanwhile, the steamroller just rolled over Quebec, driven by someone who knew what he wanted and how to get it, and who was familiar with the essence of *realpolitik*. Pierre Trudeau knew that, inside the rough shell of Quebec's claims, the centre had the consistency of fudge.

All the political rights ever gained by Quebec were acquired after it raised its voice: bilingualism in Ottawa, relative unilingualism in Quebec, the right to withdraw from joint programs, and even the space agency in Montreal. What does raising one's voice mean? It means having the right cards in one's vestpocket.

In Quebec's pocket, there was nothing. Blocking constitutional reform did not stop the country from working and Ottawa from doing as it pleased. In 1970 and 1973, voters chose a clearly federalist party. In 1976, they elected a sovereigntist party (with 41 percent of the ballots cast) that was committed not to do anything about its *raison d'être* until it had held a referendum, the first of its kind in Canadian history. Meanwhile, the balance sheet of federalism was beginning to favour Quebec (see Chapter 9).

The advent of the Parti Québécois in power caused a wave of panic in English Canada. It was just another indication that Quebecers and English Canadians constitute two nations who know next to nothing about each other.

In fact, the Parti Québécois had consistently led in public opinion polls during the eighteen months preceding the election of November 15, 1976. The reason was that federalists could support it. René Lévesque, the most popular politician in Quebec, had defined the referendum provision that the PQ had adopted in 1974 in a way they found immensely reassuring. In spite of this, the party failed to get a majority of francophone votes. (The history of constituency voting systems like ours shows that results in seats either mask or exaggerate shifts in votes.)

In the two weeks following the election, the overpriced Canadian dollar lost six cents on exchange markets, regaining three in December. After a while, people were having second thoughts about the election.

The constitutional cottage industry was bound to prosper during the political interlude between November 15, 1976 and May 20, 1980. Everywhere the cry was heard: the constitution is archaic and needs to be changed so that it recognizes the specific character of Quebec. The train of constitutional meditation stopped at every station. Even Pierre Trudeau felt he had to salute it: he set up the Commission on Canadian Unity, chaired by Jean-Luc Pépin, a former Liberal cabinet minister, and John Robarts, the former Conservative premier of Ontario. They were heavyweights in the Canadian establishment. Their report attracted the limelight when it was published in January 1979. The Quebec Liberal Party being eager to climb aboard, its then leader, Claude Ryan, issued a Beige Paper, *A New Canadian Federation*, in January 1980.

The first report proposed curbing Ottawa's spending power, establishing the statutory equality of the two levels of government and adjusting the division of powers, but without going into details. The second, besides calling for a return to the constitution of 1867, suggested changes that would enlarge provincial authority.

There was one little problem. The provinces were clearly favoured by these proposals. However, even with complete unanimity, they would be powerless if the federal government refused to listen. Ottawa might have been more attentive if faced with a real crisis, but there was none. Hence the failure of the 1978–79 constitutional talks.

All these decentralizers were kept busy distributing advice here and there. They would have been well inspired to listen themselves, just in case. Pierre Trudeau used the 1979 campaign, which he felt was his last, to talk about Canadian unity. He clearly indicated that, in the event of victory, he would give the provinces one year to reach an agreement with Ottawa on the patriation issue, failing which the people of Canada would be called upon to decide the issue in a national referendum. The outcome would almost certainly allow him to bring his unilateral patriation plans to a successful conclusion.[1] It was not the first time he had raised the possibility.

However, at the beginning of 1979, Trudeau was a lame duck. The word was, the situation would improve with a more flexible prime minister. So why should Quebecers fear the worst, even though the Pépin-Robarts Report diverged noticeably from Claude Ryan's Beige Paper? Even after Trudeau's surprise return, they were told not to worry. The priority, after all, was to overcome René Lévesque.

Without explaining what they would do if constitutional talks failed again, all these reasonable people came to Quebec asking voters to say No to the referendum question on May 20 1980. It was a fudged question, of course, but virtually everyone went underneath it and debated the straightforward issue of sovereignty.*

The authors of the question were counting on a tactical vote, something practised by only a small minority of voters. But everything has already been said on this question drafted by intellectuals. A question with suspenders and a parachute will not necessarily convince voters that there is little risk involved. It is of course difficult for people whose future is assured to understand the fear tomorrow inspires among those who do not share this feeling of security.**

A Normal Score

We shall not rehash the whole referendum campaign. However, the final result was hardly abnormal. In the first place, non-francophones — 18 percent of the population — massively mobilized in favour of the No. The country of their heart is called Canada, not Quebec. It is incredibly naive to think they might be persuaded to change their minds. In the second place, francophones were equally divided between

---

* The question read:

The government of Quebec has made public its proposal to negotiate a new agreement with the rest of Canada, based on the equality of nations;

This agreement would enable Quebec to acquire the exclusive power to make its laws, levy its taxes and establish relations abroad — in other words, sovereignty — and at the same time, to maintain with Canada an economic association including a common currency;

No change in political status resulting from these negotiations will be effected without approval by the people through another referendum;

On these terms, do you give the government of Quebec the mandate to negotiate the proposed agreement between Quebec and Canada?

Yes/No

** The best anecdote I heard about the referendum campaign is a marvelous illustration of the cleavage between the two camps. Seeing that their elderly mother would be voting No for fear of losing her old age pension, her children offered to guarantee in writing any future financial loss. Her answer was simple and disarming: "You won't even be able to keep your promise and I don't want my vote to be the cause of your impoverishment."

their roots and their fear of the economic consequences of a victory for the Yes.

The No side exploited this fear, for which they have been much blamed. Even the federal government's intervention met with condemnation, though it was perfectly legitimate since Quebec had not yet separated. The problem in this respect was the *scope* of Ottawa's intervention, which was not subject to any legislative restraints. It illustrates the asymmetrical character of Canadian federalism: the provincial government is powerless to put limits on the action of the federal government, Crown corporations, and industries under federal jurisdiction.

The manner of a campaign conveys a definite meaning. The use of fear, in April and May 1980, had a dual significance. It revealed that the simple feeling of belonging to Canada could not sway voters to the No side. For most people in Quebec, the union with Canada was a marriage of convenience rather than of love, which explains the importance given to the groom's contribution. In 1980, there was a real contribution, which the No side played up endlessly.

In fact, during those years, Quebec was receiving from the federal government $2 billion more than it paid out in taxes. By refusing to acknowledge it in 1980, Quebec was putting itself in a vulnerable position. Ottawa could choose its targets: the elderly, the unemployed, automobile owners (because of the oil equalization payments made at the time). All the steamroller had to do was to start rolling.

For all of those years of debate on the merits of federalism, the Quebec government was indulging in financial contortions that Nadia Comaneci would have envied. It was for a good cause, they said. But it deprived the provincial government of a credible response to a federal campaign based on the idea of profitable federalism.* For example, it could have insisted on the "cyclical" character of Ottawa's

*A slogan used by Robert Bourassa during his first period as premier, from 1970 to 1976.

positive contribution (the oil equalization payments could last only a short time anyway) and on the wasteful nature of antagonistic federalism.

The result might not have been different, but the way defeat was acknowledged would have been. Instead of resigning himself to defeat, René Lévesque might have said that night: "In spite of unprecedented federal expenditures in Quebec during the last few years, the reasons for which are obvious, half of the francophones in Quebec have rejected this costly duplication of Quebec resources. Obviously, we were hoping for more, but this is a solid base, which strengthens our hopes for the future and which inspires us to continue building our house in Quebec. Till next time!"

Even René Lévesque missed this unique opportunity of speaking for History. In fact, on this day of May 20, 1980, Quebecers collectively lowered their voice.

The Day After

So where did Quebec stand on the morning of May 21? René Lévesque had given no indication of what he would do in case of defeat. But he could not demand any more from Ottawa than his predecessors, and the results were known in advance. On this fundamental question he would have failed like all the others. Nevertheless, with Bill 101, he had clearly accelerated the linguistic trends, which allowed francophones to take over the jobs of anglophones leaving Quebec, or to upgrade their businesses, often with the active support of the Caisse de dépôt et placement. The results would become apparent later in the decade.

The time had not yet arrived for the final discussion with English Canada. But the building of Quebec would go on. The embers of nationalism were still smouldering, but everyone was taking defeat calmly. After all, the house was not on fire. One had to accept the rules of the game. And wasn't it spring?

However, someone was waiting in the wings, and he was in a great hurry. On May 21 1980, Jean Chrétien knocked on Claude Morin's door.[2]

The day after the referendum, the most spectacular piece of *realpolitik* in Canada's history began, "a never-seen-before demon of raw prime ministerial power," in the words of two Toronto journalists.[3] Trudeau understood the situation was ripe for striking at the very heart of the labyrinthine constitutional debate. He would do it according to his own principles and, if need be, by going over the heads of the provinces.

A great deal has been written about Pierre Trudeau's referendum promise, that a victory for the No would be interpreted as a mandate to change the constitution and revitalize Canadian federalism. The majority of voters in Quebec interpreted the promise in a radically different way than its author, and the fact exposes the gap that always existed between Trudeau and Quebec, in spite of his electoral successes.

But one must see the political meaning of this promise. In spite of appearances, it was not meant as a last-ditch effort to snatch victory on behalf of the No side. On the evening of May 14, 1980, when Trudeau committed himself, victory was already certain and the Yes was dropping in the polls. In other words, a majority of the people of Quebec preferred the calm waters of the status quo to the turbulence of sovereignty-association.

Had Trudeau resorted to the usual platitudes ("We'll work hard to improve this large and beautiful country"), he would never have had his mandate to become the "Father of the New Confederation." The operation he had in mind required the solemn commitment of May 14, which was addressed to the rest of the country in addition to Quebec.

With 74 out of a possible 75 Liberal members from Quebec in Ottawa, with the referendum results all but emasculating the government of Quebec as voters took away its freedom of action, with the federal involvement in the referendum playing a decisive and widely acknowledged role, Pierre Trudeau could turn on the ignition of the patriation steamroller.

Trudeau anticipated the failure of the preliminary talks with the provinces during the summer of 1980. On October 2, therefore, he announced that he would introduce a resolution in the House of Commons asking the British Parliament to send the Canadian constitution to Canada, with a Charter of Rights incorporating linguistic rights in the field of education. As regards the amending formula, the federal government would pursue discussions with the provinces for another two years. In case of disagreement, a national referendum would be held to allow the Canadian people to choose between a proposed federal formula, founded on a regional veto, and one advanced by the provinces as a group.[4]

This was Pierre Trudeau's renewed federalism. The Quebec Liberal Party was stunned. Some accused him of treason. But it was rather late in the day. Not only did Quebec gain nothing but the Charter took away one of its powers in education, an area reserved to the provinces. Only Ontario backed Ottawa then. New Brunswick eventually climbed aboard.

It is likely that this unilateral move helped strengthen the Parti Québécois, which used the defense of Quebec as one of the major themes of its election campaign in March and April 1981. René Lévesque pocketed an undoubted mandate to oppose Pierre Trudeau.

One Night in November

Who stopped the federal steamroller? There was nothing the first ministers of the eight dissident provinces could do. As far as Ottawa was concerned, the provinces' veto was merely a convention with no legal foundation; in any event, the courts had no business in what was a purely political issue.

We are here at the heart of asymmetrical federalism: the federal government may refer any contentious problem to the Supreme Court, yet the provinces must first apply to their own appeal courts. Time seemed to favour Ottawa.

It was Joe Clark and the Conservatives who derailed the well-laid-out strategy of the Trudeau team. To do that, they completely paralyzed the operations of the House of Commons during March and April 1981, until the government agreed to wait for the Supreme Court's decision on the legality of the patriation project.

The decision, the most eagerly awaited in Canadian history, was made public on September 28, 1981. It cut across the issue: strictly speaking, the federal project was legal but it did not conform to constitutional convention. A more substantive provincial consent was necessary. The decision was considered a relative victory for the provinces, which Ottawa admitted implicitly by convening one last meeting to see if an acceptable compromise might be in the making.

The decision might have been expected to cast a pall of gloom over Quebec, since the judges had talked of substantial rather than unanimous agreement. In this context, it was impossible to claim that Quebec had a veto, even if only founded on convention and tradition, unless one believed it was the only provincial government to have one. It would have meant stretching the concept of "two nations" to its ultimate limit. The following year, the Supreme Court did in fact reject Quebec's claim in this respect.

In other words, the foundations of Quebec's whole strategy for the previous twenty years suddenly crumbled. In 1965 and again in 1971, Quebec had blocked constitutional agreements. Now that weapon was gone.

Quebec had joined seven other dissident provinces in opposing Ottawa. This was the so-called Gang of Eight. During the last round of negotiations, in November 1981, the common front came apart bit by bit. During the evening of November 4, the day before the close of the conference, there emerged a compromise supported by every province save Quebec. In fact, there were two successive compromises. In the first, several provinces, opposed to a referendum on a constitutional amending formula, indicated that if Trudeau accepted the formula put forward by the eight provinces, they could live with a Charter of Rights enshrined in the constitution.

This so-called Vancouver formula put all of the provinces on an equal footing. To amend most clauses of the constitution, it was necessary to have the consent of the federal government and of seven provinces representing at least half the Canadian population. Quebec accepted the formula in exchange for the right of a dissident province to withdraw with full financial compensation whenever some jurisdiction was being transferred to the federal government. The amount of the compensation was to be equivalent to what federal expenditures would have been had that province agreed to the transfer.

This way Quebec did not prevent English Canada from moving in the direction of greater centralization, if that was what it wanted. At the same time it was protecting its own jurisdictions. The Vancouver compromise constituted a partial and disguised limitation of the federal government's spending power, one of the long-standing objectives of Quebec policy. And if divergences occurred over the years, Quebec would gradually acquire a special status. Trudeau said it was "separatism à la carte" and flatly rejected it on principle.

A second compromise formula was thus worked out. The Charter of Rights would include a "notwithstanding" clause allowing any province to avoid being subject to some of its provisions, if it so chose. The effect would be to moderate any loss of power by the provincial legislatures to the courts. Simultaneously, the clause relating to financial compensation would be taken out of the amending formula.

Such were the results of frantic bargaining sessions

conducted during that last night between small groups. At breakfast, Quebec was presented with a *fait accompli*.

Two factors help explain the isolation of Quebec. First, public opinion in English Canada was pushing the provinces into being part of the noble enterprise of cutting the last legal links with Britain. As soon as certain members of the Gang of Eight began responding to federal overtures, the situation was transformed. One thing leading to another, a web of isolation was woven around Quebec. No anglophone province wanted to be in a position of turning down Canada for Quebec, especially a Quebec with a "separatist" leader.

But why not have told Quebec about the deals being cut? Because the provinces were eager for an agreement and were ready to compromise. They knew that René Lévesque had gambled everything on the common declaration of the Gang of Eight on April 16, 1981, and that it was as far as he would ever go. But he was helpless, because the Supreme Court decision had just undercut Quebec's claim to a veto.

In the end, however, the second factor would carry the day. A Canadian prime minister from an anglophone province would never have been able to treat Quebec in such a manner. But Pierre Trudeau draped himself in his referendum promise and his referendum victory. What anglophone would dare contradict his claim to be more representative of Québec than René Lévesque? This argument of legitimacy carried the remaining "hold-out" provinces of English Canada.[5] The Quebec Liberal Party hardly caused a ripple by supporting Lévesque in rejecting the new constitutional accord.

Quebecers, crafty enough to avoid putting all of their eggs in the same basket, woke up on the morning of November 5, 1981, to one of the most pitiful omelets in their history.

The Scene After the Battle

What Quebec remembers of the night of November 5 are the long knives and the inclusion in the Charter of Rights of a clause guaranteeing Canadian anglophones access to English-language schools in Quebec. But this last was a minor element in the debate. As for the long knives, they may have cut into Quebec's pride but otherwise had little political significance. Even if Quebec's delegation had been informed minute by minute of the bargaining between Ottawa and the other provinces, it would not have changed the completely unacceptable character of the ultimate compromise. But one can't go on saying over and over again that the fundamental interests of Quebec and English Canada are divergent and then express surprise at having been right.

The truth of the matter is that Quebec is seriously weakened by the new amending formula. And one must keep in mind that it was Quebec that asked for these interminable constitutional discussions. It was Quebec that called for a formula to put an end to federal intrusions in provincial jurisdiction as well as a new division of powers. It was then understood that its veto would be preserved in some form or other.

As it turned out, there was no new division of powers — the accord of November 1981 reinforced provincial rights over non-renewable resources, which affected mainly the western provinces. In addition, there was no limitation on the federal spending power, and Quebec could no longer prevent a transfer of power from the provinces to the federal government if supported by Ottawa and seven provinces with more than 50 percent of the population.

The amending formula allows any province to refuse such a transfer and continue exercising its own jurisdiction. But, without fiscal compensation, taxpayers in that province are penalized: part of their federal taxes go to pay for the new federal program in those provinces agreeing to a transfer of jurisdiction. Meanwhile, consenting provinces would be able to spend tax revenue on other programs of their own. Compensation would be available for opting out only if powers dealing with education and culture were transferred to the federal government.

Did Quebec grasp the magnitude of its defeat? *In November 1981, the federal government agreed to consolidate in the Constitution the very process that pushed Quebec to seek its revision in the first place.* In other words, the constitution of 1982 enables the federal government to take over provincial jurisdictions bit by bit (save for education and culture), as long as the anglophone majority agrees. At every stage, Quebec can be isolated just as it was with shared-cost programs in the fifties and sixties. The new provision comes on top of the declaratory* and spending powers of the federal government with which it can trim provincial authority.

In November 1981, Canada did not go back to square one. In fact, it destroyed the old illusion that the two levels of government were somehow equal. For Quebec, insult was added to injury: with the new amending formula, Quebec has *less* power than the four Atlantic provinces combined, which have less than a third of its population.

A constitution lasts a long time, and this one has been solidly locked up, as we shall see. Its authors, Pierre Trudeau and company, said that, in any event, Quebec would be protected by its political weight and that never would anyone dare play such tricks. Yet this is precisely what happened in November 1981.

There is a supreme irony here. In 1965, Trudeau the intellectual had warned the Quebec government against the temptation of reopening the constitutional debate. Centralizers, he wrote at the time, will have the opportunity of scoring points, with Quebec as a loser.[6] Seventeen years later, Pierre Trudeau would fulfil his own prophecy.

---

*That is, the power to declare that a certain sector bears on the overall national interest, and therefore becomes part of the federal jurisdiction.

The Quest for the Magic Mandate

The author of this ambitious operation kept on claiming, on the one hand, that he had a mandate from the people and, on the other, that it is Quebec that voluntarily gave up its veto.[7] What must one think of this?

Every elected government has a mandate to govern. The final outcome of the constitutional operation was perfectly legal. There is little to say on that score. However, one can't say Trudeau had received a mandate for this specific reform for the simple reason that it had never been submitted for popular approval.

The electoral argument, which he uses and abuses, could be turned round: three-quarters of the federal MPs from Quebec who voted in favour of the agreement of November 1981 were *defeated* in the federal election of September 1984. The argument that the election did not specifically bear on the constitution of 1982 is very tenuous: it was one of the main themes of the campaign (Brian Mulroney's speech in Sept-Iles on integrating Quebec into the constitution had a considerable effect), while it had been totally absent from the campaign in February 1980.*

Supposing, on May 14, 1980, Trudeau had said: "I solemnly undertake on the basis of a No vote to set in motion the process of constitutional reform. The new constitution will not alter the division of powers but will include a Charter of Rights allowing, among other things, Canadians from other provinces to enrol their children in English-language schools in Quebec. It will also include an amending formula that will place all the provinces on an equal footing, with no provincial vetoes and without any compensation for those who do not follow suit when other provinces are ready to

---

*Pierre Trudeau once more trotted out the argument of the February 1980 election while promoting the book *Towards a Just Society: The Trudeau Years.* He should have been laughed out of town, all the more because he was also saying that the Government of Quebec must obtain a clear mandate if it wanted to bring about independence.

transfer some of their economic and social prerogatives to the federal government. This is the renewed federalism I am offering you, and we are putting our seats at risk to bring it about." If he had said that and won, then he would have had his mandate.

Wrangling Over Quebec's Veto

At the time, the veto question provided a lot of amusement for cartoonists and orthodox federalists, who misrepresented the events leading to its ultimate resolution.

When René Lévesque formally traded Quebec's veto, which he believed it had, for an amending formula offering opting out with full compensation in the new constitution, he was not giving up his veto with respect to the operation in progress. The veto would lapse only with the adoption of the new constitution.[8]

This is elementary common sense. A union agreement remains in force until the date specified in the contract, even though the union leadership may decide, for the new contract, to trade some advantageous clause for compensatory gains elsewhere. It is as if the employer, in the final bargaining sprint, refused to accept the improvements and at the same time did away with the clause the union was ready to give up, saying the union did not feel it was important anyway. This is exactly what happened with Quebec's veto.

Had the Supreme Court ruled that some provinces, including Quebec, had a veto, there is no doubt at all that Quebec would have exercised that right on the morning of November 5, 1981. But such was not the case.

It must be said that it was not Trudeau who fought against the idea of a veto for certain provinces, including Quebec. He always favoured the so-called Victoria amending formula. It stipulated that any amendment should receive the consent of the federal government, Quebec, Ontario, two of the four Atlantic provinces, and two of the four western provinces. Few provinces agreed with this formula.

Moreover, since the veto was not presented as a central political issue by Quebec, the final rounds of bargaining were that much easier for Trudeau.

There are two questions arising out of Trudeau's attitude. The first concerns the curious asymmetry behind it. He claimed to represent Quebec voters for *all* questions under discussion, save the amending formula where he took shelter behind a fragment of Quebec's position (letting go of the veto). Curious, indeed!

The second question concerns the significance of this attitude. There is one obvious conclusion to be drawn from the way the constitutional talks unfolded: Quebec was the *only* important province to which Trudeau gave nothing in return for something. He refused to impose bilingualism on Ontario's Parliament and courts, even though Quebec had had it since Confederation. He gave the western provinces a "notwithstanding" clause allowing them to get around certain provisions of the Charter of Rights, accepted the amending formula they preferred, and strengthened their authority over natural resources on their territory.

He did not intervene at the end to declare: "Gentlemen, you have all won something during this long night, so wouldn't it be normal that my own province should also get something? Let us ignore René Lévesque, who is sulking. What we are dealing with are the superior interests of Quebec and of Canada. Men may come and men may go, but a constitution goes on. We will all make one last leap of imagination and find some way of providing Quebec with some sort of implicit veto. What would you say if we replaced the 50 percent requirement in the amending formula with 75 percent?" (At the time, Quebec had 26 percent of the Canadian population.)

It is rather surprising that, after having so often endorsed the theory of counterweights, Trudeau did not seek to protect Quebec in one way or another. The fact is that he fought resolutely for minority language rights but did not budge on the issue of Quebec's veto. This is the essence of Trudeau. The only possible conclusion is that he considered Quebec a province like any other, so that the second point was not as important as the first.

One objection may be that Trudeau couldn't have brought the English-speaking provinces on side. If so, in spite of unusually favourable circumstances, it means simply that a French-speaking prime minister, even at the top of his form and his power, was incapable of protecting the vital interests of his own province.

At the very end, would an alliance between Quebec and Ottawa have salvaged Quebec's veto? In fact, there existed, for a few hours, a feeling that such an alliance was taking shape. The other dissident provinces were not amused. It was quickly realized that the whole manoeuvre was meant to break up the Gang of Eight, which was already rather shaky. The scheme worked and, in the process, freed them from their association with Quebec. Eight years later, Jean Chrétien was still laughing.[9]

Quebec thus lost its birthright. But there was worse to come.

The Member for Montmorency

In English Canada, no one, or hardly anyone, was offended by Quebec's defeat. Yet there was a very noisy campaign to restore to the Charter the clauses relating to native people and sexual equality that had been lost in the shuffle. When the final resolution came up in the House of Commons on December 2, 1981, a single Liberal from Quebec, among 74, invoked the way the constitution had been imposed on Quebec and voted against it: Louis Duclos, the member for Montmorency. A few Liberal and Conservative senators, including Lowell Murray, had the same reaction.

Such a gesture involves fewer risks for a senator who enjoys tenure. Louis Duclos was immediately blacklisted: no more missions abroad, no more committee chairs. Even in democratic countries, History can be unjust. In the election of September 1984, Duclos suffered the same fate as the large majority of his Liberal colleagues and was submerged by the Tory tide. It is an additional proof that the tactical vote is not part of our heritage.

Yet, during these melancholy days, there was at least one Liberal in Ottawa who remembered his roots.

The Parti Québécois Circus

Meanwhile in Quebec, reason seemed to have lost its hold. The government was under heavy fire for its bargaining strategy and its positions before the federal steamroller. All of this is debatable, but could it have acted differently? The government's weakness came from the results of the referendum. However, the same government had a mandate from the election of April 1981 to defend the best interests of Quebec.

It was after the constitutional debacle, and not before, that the shoe began pinching, because there was still one way out for the government. Instead, Quebec politics turned into a circus in a way never seen before.

After the pitiable return from Ottawa of the Quebec delegation, we saw the unprecedented spectacle of a ruling party losing control of its own convention as a result of, among other things, the verbal excesses of its leader, the premier of Quebec. And then the leader compelled his followers, including cabinet ministers, to kneel publicly and praise him so that he would be persuaded to remain at his post. Nothing like this had ever been seen in Western countries, although such a personality cult is practised in other political systems.

The climax of the Parti Québécois circus was the decision to hold a referendum among the rank and file. To reverse the decisions of that wretched convention, which had radicalized the party program in the direction of sovereignty, the leader asked members to cast a ballot by mail.

It is not unreasonable to say that, during those few days, the supporters of sovereignty had all lost their heads, except one: Pierre Bourgault.[10] René Lévesque won that referendum. However, it was the start of the Parti Québécois's self-inflicted mutilation, and there was not a single Louis Duclos to challenge this sorry spectacle.

Without going as far as saying that such was its intended strategy, the circus diverted attention from the stinging constitutional defeat suffered at the hands of Pierre Trudeau and from the response that should have been prepared. Because there were other ways to reply besides sulking and rattling cages.

We have seen that Trudeau, contrary to his claims, had no mandate from the people for his constitutional operation. That was the opening through which anger could have been channeled, allowing Parti Québécois members to let off steam, by calling a general election on the issue. The theme pursued by the Parti Québécois could have been: "Either we obtain recognition of Quebec's rights (for instance, the veto or the right of opting out with financial compensation) or we launch the process leading up to independence."

Public opinion polls at the time show that a victory for the Parti Québécois was not out of the question. It would have been a close fight anyway, with nationalist elements in the Liberal Party up against the wall. Whatever the outcome of the vote, it would have been an embarrassment for the federal government. The demands of a Liberal government, as seen from the party platform, were not softer than those of the Parti Québécois.[11]

The other provinces would have been in a delicate situation. They would have had to assess the impact of their decisions, rather than being content with the thought that Trudeau wanted them to keep in mind: *Pierre Trudeau really did the separatists in, didn't he?* His legitimacy would have been seriously eroded. To the point of bending to Quebec? One can't possibly know, but the Parti Québécois would at least have transformed a historic defeat into a courageous response, thereby taking the initiative away from the federal government.

Clearly, the election could have been lost. It is hard to give up power, even when the higher interests of Quebec are at stake. But inaction was the worst possible solution: it turned Trudeau's operation into a rather commonplace event, conferring legitimacy by default ("If you don't react, then it can't be all that terrible!"). Yet the same government, a year later, aroused the hostility of its closest allies, wage-earners in the public and parapublic service, thereby giving up any chance of winning the next general election. In effect it imposed temporary but substantial cuts in their salaries (with the exception of low-income earners), in order to contain the ballooning provincial deficits. According to the government, this kamikaze operation was justified on the basis of "Quebec's higher interests."

Failure to even contemplate the possibility of a general election in 1981 shows the government's disarray. The good government of 1976–81 had become a government of boy scouts. Intuition indeed has its limits in politics. Oh! If only a Pierre Trudeau had been leading Quebec at the time...

CHAPTER 6

Meech Lake: When Moderation Tastes No Better

Canada had renewed its constitution, which was now framed and in the parlour. For the first time it was pure maple leaf. However, one signature was lacking, and not a negligable one. It was an embarrassment, all the more so in that Quebecers were determined not to let things be. Federalists had taken over from "separatists" in Quebec City, but their demands, even if more moderate, seemed substantial enough.

Prosperity had returned, as well as some old "new" players, and in September 1984, the remnants of the Trudeau team were given early retirement by the voters. So why not make another effort, a constitutional one, to get Quebec's missing signature at the bottom of that new sheepskin?

Such a Short Cease-fire

Let us recapitulate. At the beginning of 1986, Quebec was in a worse situation than in 1965 as regards its constitutional place in Confederation. However, calm had returned on the language front, even though a number of cases relative to the commercial signs disposition in Bill 101 were winding their way through the court system. The new Liberal government was upholding Bill 101 while offering concessions to anglophones without provoking a backlash. Was a durable linguistic peace in sight?

A new guard was rising, in tune with the stock market. Quebec was in love with business. People realized that there were fewer problems in the acquisition and management of business firms than in understanding the mysteries of the Catholic Church. How thrilling to discover that two and two make four, *even in French*, that people named Tremblay and Gagnon could take over large companies, canvass foreign markets, all with the help of the Quebec government. It was and it still is quite a revolution. Within fifteen years, Quebecers had taken over several economic sectors and made impressive gains in banking and finance.

During that period, there also was a critical transformation in the Quebec view of federal elections. The constitutional disaster of 1981 certainly had something to do with it. Until then, Quebecers were confident that their federal leaders would never be deceitful, even though they growled at the provincial government. That was thought to be part of the game of flexible federalism. They were seen as promoting Quebec's interests on the large federal rink. It was the rule of double legitimacy.

The bitter lesson of 1981 was not forgotten. But was there a way out? It is not enough to vote against someone; one must have the impression of voting *for* someone representing a potential improvement. The nature of the alternative was somewhat ironic. In June 1983, Brian Mulroney took over a party that, in Quebec, was more like a particle.

Mulroney had campaigned on the No side in the referendum and supported Trudeau's constitutional approach in 1980 and 1981,[1] and harshly attacked the separatists during his leadership campaign in the spring of 1983. Yet he was the instrument of nationalism's revenge. He had no problem supporting Quebec nationalism to defeat the Liberals in Quebec, the only region where they showed any strength. It was all the easier to do since Trudeau had just left politics. The rest of Canada was much too busy getting rid of its own Liberals to care in the least about what was brewing in Quebec. For the average Conservative, anyway, Quebec was about as familiar as Finland.

At the start of the 1984 election campaign, absolutely no one had anticipated the final results in Quebec. And yet people say that election campaigns don't really change anything! Sovereigntists and nationalists jostled at the door of the Conservative Party, encouraged by John Turner's disastrous campaign. The night of the election, only four Liberals were left in French Quebec (seventeen in all of Quebec).* Quebecers had just traded *French Power* for *Quebec Power.*

"What are you going to do for Quebec?" became the only relevant issue. For the first time, there would be a large *Québec bloc* in Parliament. (The Bloc Populaire had pursued a similar goal with little success during the forties. It was solely a Quebec party.) Without a commanding idea, the vaunted Liberal machine was an empty shell. Contrary to the conventional wisdom, it is ideas that generate political organizations in a democratic society, and not the reverse.

Was there anyone in 1982 who imagined that people from the Yes side in the referendum would be taking their place in the *Canadian* government? In 1984, it was an accomplished fact. These former sovereigntists (Suzanne Blais-Grenier, Benoît Bouchard, Monique Landry, Monique

---

* The 1984 election in Quebec provides the ultimate proof of the non-existence of the tactical vote. The collapse of the Liberal Party across Canada provided the NDP with an unprecedented opportunity. If the party had discreetly encouraged its supporters to vote Conservative in Quebec's urban ridings, even fewer Liberals would have been elected. In eleven Quebec ridings, the Liberal majority over the Conservative candidate was much less than the number of NDP votes. As the Liberal Party won only forty seats across Canada to the NDP's thirty, these eleven ridings would have allowed the NDP to become the official Opposition in the House of Commons. The political dynamics in Canada would have been transformed. Partisan politics often wins out over a party's true interest.

Vézina, Lucien Bouchard joined on in 1988) had assumed the responsibility for patching things up.

The new constitutional cloth was cut faster than anyone would have thought. In May 1986, the new Liberal government in Quebec published its five conditions for adhering to the Canadian constitution. On April 30, 1987, after many bilateral discussions, a meeting of the eleven heads of government took place at Meech Lake. To everyone's surprise, the meeting unanimously endorsed a text incorporating Quebec's five conditions. Legal experts were asked to redraft it as a constitutional resolution. Another meeting was set for June 2 in Ottawa. Only late in the night was unanimity achieved.[2] The new constitutional resolution was introduced that same day in the House of Commons. The prime minister and the premiers had promised to act diligently.

A triumphant drumroll would bring Quebec back into the constitution and erase the wrongs of 1981–82. The future looked bright, with no constitutional clouds in sight. Even English Canada seemed rather happy about the whole business.

Unfortunately, thunder had already sounded. A few days earlier, the departed leader had come down from his mountain, like an unwanted Cincinnatus, to lead the charge. On May 27, 1987, Pierre Trudeau published a vitriolic attack against the draft of the Meech Lake Accord.[3] The truce was at an end.

The Quintessence of Meech

Is it possible to get at the heart of the countless comments, articles, and replies that have poured forth during the last three years? Can one make a coherent presentation of all the radically divergent interpretations? How is it that, in spite of a flood of ink, so many elementary errors persist?

The Meech Lake Accord incorporates the five conditions that Quebec put forward in May 1986. But we should note, first of all, that Meech has been subject to much abuse and misuse of language. It is said, for example, that the accord would allow the integration of Quebec into the constitution of 1982. However, it makes substantial changes to the constitution, precisely to satisfy Quebec. Meech was just as bold in its design as the patriation operation.

The five conditions set by Quebec bear on the following points:[4]

1. The explicit recognition of Quebec as a distinct society;

2. The guarantee of additional powers in the area of immigration;

3. The limitation of the federal spending power;

4. The granting of a veto on future institutional changes;

5. Quebec participation in the appointment of Supreme Court justices originating from Quebec.

How do these five conditions relate to the issues of the past thirty years? The third and fourth conditions modify the 1981 amending formula, which deprived Quebec of any protection for its economic and social jurisdictions. The formula incorporated into the Meech Lake Accord conforms fairly closely to the one accepted by the eight dissident provinces in April 1981.

The formula provides for financial compensation for *all* provincial powers that dissident provinces may refuse to transfer to the federal government. On the other hand, it requires unanimity for any change in federal institutions. In the constitution of 1982, the powers of the Senate, the selection of its members, and the establishment of new provinces (in the Northwest Territories or the Yukon) come under the general amending formula (seven provinces with 50 percent of the population).

Therefore, the damage inflicted in 1981 was repaired. In addition, Quebec put forward some of its earlier demands, which meant more powers for the province than had been available before 1982. Thus, any province could opt out of any new joint program launched by Ottawa in areas of provincial jurisdiction, and it would also receive financial compensation inasmuch as it implemented a program "compatible with national objectives."

However, the division of powers, the subject of Quebec's demands since 1965, was not on the agenda. The grey areas of the original British North America Act persist, except for immigration, where Quebec received additional powers and related revenues. Quebec is also empowered to choose, jointly with the federal government, future senators and three judges of the Supreme Court who must be from Quebec.

Finally, the Meech Lake Accord inserts in the constitution an interpretive clause defining the linguistic duality of Canada and recognizing the distinctive character of Quebec society. And the Quebec government has an obligation to *promote* this distinctiveness.

Quebec's Gains

THE DISTINCT SOCIETY

The clauses on the distinct society have caused the most controversy. Their effect is difficult to gauge because of their general character. According to Pierre Trudeau, they provide Quebec with a special status enabling it to claim more and more powers in the future, as new areas not specified in the present division of powers come to the fore. It would eventually tiptoe out of Confederation.

Such an interpretation is understandable in a *political* perspective: the clause would whet Quebec's appetite and trigger escalating demands. However, from a legal point of view, the distinct society clause specifies: "Nothing in this section derogates from the powers, rights or privileges of Parliament or the Government of Canada, or of the legislature of governments of the provinces."[5] Logically, this restriction should apply to all future areas not yet specified in the present division of powers. Yet this is precisely the basis of

Trudeau's legal arguments on the distinct society clause.[6] Hence, Trudeau's position lacks substance. Moreover, there is no procedure enabling any *one* province to demand and obtain additional powers. This would require a constitutional amendment in due form, with the consent of the federal government. To date, this has never occurred.

Those in English Canada who are inclined to support the distinct society clause generally say that its effect will be minimal. Its opponents say the contrary — and they have scored points by saying so. It seems more reasonable to believe that the clause consolidates Quebec's linguistic powers, notably with respect to immigration. In other words, it would give Quebec more elbow room in its own jurisdictions.

One example comes to mind. The Supreme Court recognized in its celebrated decision on the sign law, in December 1988, that the Charter and hence the constitution did not prevent Quebec from *imposing* French signs on its territory. It would be very surprising if the Supreme Court allowed an anglophone province to impose English signs. The Quebec context was taken into account.

The accord implicitly limits the scope of the distinct society clause in a way that has so far gone largely unnoticed: *each of the powers devolved upon Quebec is also devolved upon the other provinces.* This special status has a funny ring to it.

Should Quebec take offence because it has no special status as regards the supplementary powers devolved upon the provinces? What matters is the content, not the container. Quebec does not need to feel diminished because other provinces participate in the choice of justices of the Supreme Court and senators who represent them in the Upper House. In 1979, the Pépin-Robarts *Report on Canadian Unity* noted that Canada, among federal countries, had been most careful in not giving the Upper House the role of protector of regional interests against federal legislation.[7] In other words, the provinces, when in Ottawa's path, were rather powerless within the present federal system.

It is difficult to see how Quebec might be harmed by the expanded role of the provinces. Obviously, their nominees would be people sympathetic to their aims. However, it is Ottawa's choice, based on a provincial list. The accord has no procedure for reconciling fundamental disagreements. It is an oversight, but nothing prevents the federal government from asking to see a second list, or even a third one. It is noteworthy that none of the dissident provinces — New Brunswick, Manitoba, and Newfoundland — seemed to worry about this.

Another point also seems to have escaped notice. The accord says that the Canadian Parliament has the role of preserving Canadian duality, of which the French character of Quebec is a major element. Parliament could therefore intervene to defend this character, which never was a priority with Pierre Trudeau. Why not require, for example, that all federal employees working regularly in Quebec be able to get along in French? This would make a difference in Hull and in Crown corporations with offices in Montreal.

The accord therefore recognizes the linguistic changes of the past twenty years in Quebec. *Unilingual* anglophones in Quebec might find it worrisome, but for the French minorities outside Quebec nothing is changed.

FEDERAL SPENDING POWER

Quebec has obtained a certain satisfaction, as regards the future, on the limitation of federal spending power in areas of provincial jurisdiction. But not for the past: existing joint programs will continue. Quebec thereby loses any chance of having Ottawa withdraw and obtaining a matching financial compensation.

However, even with this limitation, the federal government can still launch new programs in areas of exclusive provincial jurisdiction and *impose* them by using the provision of financial compensation if a majority of the provinces accept the federal intrusion. The province that opts out and refuses to launch a comparable program will penalize its citizens, whose federal taxes help pay for the new program in the consenting provinces. But then one might ask: if Ottawa pays, where is the problem?

The answer to this question is just as valid today as it was twenty-five years ago, when Jean Lesage was thundering against the Trojan horse of joint programs. Whenever, in a federal system, one level of government can intervene with its own standards and criteria in another jurisdiction, dysfunctions arise and a momentum is created that will bring about a progressive shift of power from one to the other. In other words, it goes against the spirit of federalism. Pierre Trudeau, the intellectual who thought in terms of counterweights, thought so too.

For the moment, federal authorities are weighed down by a heavy debt, inherited from the previous administration. The momentum of the debt is important. If there had been in 1984 a $180-billion debt, but only a $5-billion deficit, then a rise of 50 percent in the public debt since 1984 would have to be ascribed to the new government. Such is not the case, the deficit in 1984 was $30 billion. The question is: what would the public debt be in 1990 if the spending and fiscal structure of 1984 had been maintained throughout? Certainly higher than it is now. In this sense the present debt is a legacy. Ottawa is thus incapable of launching new and ambitious national programs. The sad saga of the national day care program says as much: the Conservatives unveiled this program a few months before the election of November 1988, only to announce its demise in the budget speech of April 1989. But constitutions have a long life, even when poorly put together, as in 1981–82. Someday, Ottawa will again have more room to manoeuvre.

What is involved here is a partial limitation of federal spending power. Had it existed in the sixties, Quebec would not have had to fight to salvage its own pension plan. But it would have been led to establish a number of programs, notably in the housing sector, which did not meet its particular needs. The accord provides a certain leeway in the norms governing a dissident province. But it would certainly not be acceptable to use funds allocated for low-cost family housing to build shelters for the homeless or spend them on adult literacy programs.

The accord does not guarantee the permanence of financial compensation, which would probably take the form of an annual transfer of funds instead of income tax points. And what if Ottawa ultimately withdraws from one of these programs? Future problems in this respect may not be very different from current ones.

Obviously, the provinces are stronger with the Meech Lake Accord than under the constitution of 1982. Canada has taken a step towards decentralization, but we are still very far from a rational and functional federalism where overlapping jurisdictions have been reduced as much as possible. In fact, not a single case of overlapping has been eliminated (except perhaps immigration); the relative inferiority of the provinces has been perpetuated. The Quebec government has referred to its conditions as minimal ones. But once the accord is ratified, it would be possible to negotiate further transfers of power. Or so it professed to believe.

Derailment

Most of the accord's critics don't want a more balanced federalism. They don't admit that the provinces should be a bit more "sovereign" within their own jurisdiction. And they are not comfortable with the concept of two nations. If they were consistent, they would call for the accord's outright rejection. But they are embarrassed by the problem of Quebec. Most of them will grant that the constitution of 1982 is unacceptable to Quebec. They don't want to give the impression of rejecting Quebec, so they keep beating around the bush. They refuse to see that Quebecers have a different view of themselves and thus refuse to admit that they too must come to a decision on the future of the country.

Opponents of the accord, aroused by Pierre Trudeau, had ample time to organize. At this point, one must clear up a widely held misconception about the constitutional timetable for amendments. The three-year span for the Meech Lake Accord expires on June 23 1990. It is a maximal limit, but not mandatory. The constitution is explicit on this point: amendments come into effect with the Royal Proclamation, which can take place as soon as the eleven legislatures have ratified a constitutional resolution. If all had acted with the same speed as Robert Bourassa, the Meech Lake Accord could have been in effect as early as the fall of 1988, taking into account the Senate's suspensive veto of 180 days on constitutional resolutions, a veto exercised by Trudeau loyalists, who are in the majority there.

Pierre Trudeau gave the anti-Meech coalition six months' breathing time. It was a rather unusual situation: the Senate supported the former leader of the party rather than the current leader, John Turner, who had voted in favour of the accord in the House of Commons.

When they signed the Meech Lake Accord, the eleven first Mministers agreed to proceed with diligence. The Canadian Parliament was scheduled to hold public hearings during the summer of 1987, and the provincial legislatures were expected to proceed quickly with a vote of ratification. The process was immediately set in motion. Robert Bourassa was even ahead of the agreed timetable: he had the accord ratified by the National Assembly on June 23, 1987, which set the constitutional clock ticking.

The question is, why did the premiers of New Brunswick and Manitoba, Richard Hatfield and Howard Pawley, fail to submit the accord to their respective legislatures? The first one chose to call an election in September 1987, before tabling the accord. His opponent, Frank McKenna, won by taking every seat in the legislature. Howard Pawley had more time, since he was not forced to call an election before April 1988. He was then defeated, and soundly so. Conservative leader Gary Filmon formed a minority government, with the official Opposition led by Liberal Sharon Carstairs, a determined opponent of the accord.

Richard Hatfield and Howard Pawley (who was very reticent) were the only ones not to follow up on their signatures.

But why? Because opponents of the accord had regrouped and managed to throw a wrench in the ratification procedure. In the absence of unanimity, it would have been unseemly to proceed too hastily. The opposition had to be given time to express itself, and, in any event, there were still three years to pull the whole thing together. Meanwhile, opposition was growing much more vocal. Attempts to derail the accord started very early on.

But let us stop for a moment and admire how Pierre Trudeau and his team managed to lock up some essential points of the constitution in 1982. The consent of the federal government and of seven provinces with half the Canadian population is all that is required for the transfer of provincial powers to the federal government. But to modify this clause and the one on the absence of financial compensation for a dissident province, not only is unanimity of the eleven governments required but it must be backed by a resolution adopted in each legislature. The whole process can stretch over three years. Any legislature may reverse its decision before the final proclamation. In this respect, the constitution of 1982 is cast in concrete.

Some invoke this situation to attack the veto wielded by each province over institutional change; it is not normal, they say, that a small province of 120,000 inhabitants (Prince Edward Island) can stall an amendment wanted by every other government. But is there an alternative without a similar quantitative bias? There are no miracle formulas for amending constitutions.

In the case of the Meech Lake failure, one must make a distinction between legal mechanisms and the political momentum behind it. Legally, it is true, a single province can torpedo the accord. Politically, though, things are very different. Were Newfoundland truly isolated, it could hardly resist the pressures of the other ten governments. The long history of constitutional repatriation efforts shows that no attempt was ever lost because of the objections of one small province.

In fact, opposition to the accord is anything but isolated. The three provinces who objected to the agreement in March 1990 had a very large audience in English Canada. This also explains the waning enthusiasm of some other provinces. The accord has turned out to be far more divisive that the accord of 1981, which received almost unanimous support outside Quebec. One can admire people like Marc Lalonde, who displayed unusual ingenuity trying to convince English Canada to scuttle the accord while telling Quebec its failure was attributable to only 6 percent of the Canadian population!

The election of Gary Filmon in Manitoba, in May 1988, marked the true beginning of hostilities. The two opposition parties, the Liberals and the NDP, rejected the Meech Lake Accord: protection of language minorities left a lot to be desired, Quebec was more equal than the others, Senate reform would be hampered, and the federal government would be unable to implement national programs *a mari usque ad mare*. The opposition had a majority of the seats. Gary Filmon was pinned to the wall.

A few months later, the federal election on the free trade pact caused a formidable rise in Canadian nationalism, to which Quebec reacted with stony indifference. Quebecers even took great pleasure in tipping the scales the other way. In English Canada, the Conservatives received less than 40 percent of the votes,[8] while benefiting from a split opposition. Had Quebec voted the same way as English Canada, the free trade pact would have been defeated. This created some bitterness across Canada.

Such was the situation when Robert Bourassa tabled Bill 178, in December 1988, responding to the Supreme

Court's decision on the sign law. The bill maintained the prohibition against any language other than French for exterior signs, except for anglophone sociocultural institutions, and, to avoid a new court challenge, the government invoked the "notwithstanding clause."

Quebec was about to experience its umpteenth language psychodrama, culminating in the resignation of three anglophone ministers from the cabinet. Anger welled up in English Canada. Gary Filmon became a hero overnight by withdrawing the constitutional resolution he had just tabled before the Manitoba legislature. It sounded like the first nail in the accord's coffin.

The second nail came on April 20, 1989, as Clyde Wells became premier of Newfoundland. He is a disciple of Pierre Trudeau and never hesitated to speak out against the essential clauses of the accord. The opposition of Frank McKenna, who was simply in no hurry, paled by comparison. Meanwhile, Canadian attitudes soured and a growing number of people were turning their backs on Canadian duality. This is hardly surprising as federal leaders, ever since the early debates on bilingualism, had never come up with an alternative to the Trudeau model.

After thirty years of debate, nothing had really been solved. The language question and Quebec's place in Confederation had fused into a single issue. Having no influence over the first, English Canada would compensate with the second — while trying to save appearances.

An attempt would be made to reconcile the irreconcilable. Why not try to resolve the concerns of all in a *second* agreement, which would accompany the Meech Lake Accord?

A Perpendicular Parallel Accord?

Partisan politics took over the debate on the Meech Lake Accord, as the trial balloon of a parallel agreement shows eloquently. The section of the accord dealing with constitutional conferences is convincing in this respect: "A constitutional conference composed of the Prime Minister of Canada and the first ministers of the provinces shall be convened by the Prime Minister of Canada at least once each year.... The conferences shall have included on their agenda the following matters: a) *Senate Reform*, including the role and the functions of the Senate, its powers, the method of selecting Senators and representation in the Senate; b) roles and responsibilities in relation to fisheries; and c) such other matters as are agreed upon."[9]

In other words, if a parallel accord means agreement on the agenda of the next constitutional conference — and this was Quebec's position in mid-March 1990 — then it is totally superfluous since it is already included in the Meech Lake Accord. The three dissident provinces, however, had something else in mind: they saw a parallel agreement as a way of getting around certain clauses of the original accord or of resolving certain questions left up in the air, such as Senate reform.

The truth is as simple as it is brutal: neither Ontario nor Quebec are interested in Senate reform as proposed by the western provinces, because it would be to the advantage of the seven smaller provinces. The political influence of Quebec (which now has 23 percent of the Senate) would decline dramatically if senators were elected in equal numbers from each province and the Senate retained its present powers. It can block indefinitely any law voted by the House of Commons, except for constitutional laws.

Under the amending formula in force until ratification of the Meech Lake Accord, only one of the two central provinces must be won over for reform to go ahead. After Meech Lake, *both* Ontario and Quebec must be brought on side.

The kind of Senate reform of interest to Quebec was obtained during the Meech Lake negotiations, at Alberta's request: nominations made from a list supplied by the province are even better for Quebec than elected senators!

As of mid-March 1990, everything was blocked. No one was ready to give and Robert Bourassa had no freedom to manoeuvre. Quebecers would never understand how he could give away any more for an accord that was supposed to be only a first step and, as we know today, would block the future for quite a while.

But it was still possible to look at the failing accord in political terms rather than in simplistic moral terms (all this is Filmon's fault or Wells's fault). Contrary to the prevailing view in Quebec, there were no ethical lapses on the part of the dissident provinces. No premier can prejudge the will of his Parliament for the next three years. And don't the voters have anything to say about changes in the supreme law of the land? Nothing was done against the rules.

However, tension was rising across Canada, particularly in Quebec, which was already sending broad hints about the consequences flowing from a rejection of the accord: "Not necessarily sovereignty, but sovereignty if necessary." When historians begin probing this tragicomical period, they will be surprised to see that there was nobody on the other end of the line. English Canada was out to lunch.

No one in Quebec had anticipated the thunderclap of March 22, 1990. The previous day, the government of New Brunswick had tabled *two* constitutional resolutions, one relating to the Meech Lake Accord and the other enumerating the requisites for New Brunswick's acceptance of the accord, which were to be ratified fairly quickly after June 23, 1990. The idea was to launch at once a second round of constitutional negotiations, even though Quebec had long insisted that it must sign the constitution before joining a new round of talks. But there was worse: the second resolution contained two major modifications to the Meech Lake Accord. And Premier Frank McKenna was supposed to be the most moderate of the three dissidents!

A simple bargaining stance? The next day, March 22,

Brian Mulroney solemnly announced to the nation that New Brunswick's position was a good starting position. He was dropping his friend Robert Bourassa and Quebec, his province. Furthermore, there would be public hearings before a committee of the House of Commons, all groups and organizations being welcome with their suggestions. Knowing what English Canada thought of Meech Lake...

Brian Mulroney seemed ready to surrender to public opinion in English Canada. It was perhaps inevitable, but in the process he was opening a Pandora's box. It contained one affliction fatal to Quebec: the constitution of 1982.

The provinces of English Canada, each with a shopping list, would conduct their own negotiations, amend the Meech Lake Accord, and even amend the present constitution, if they could agree among themselves. Obviously there was no guarantee that the prime minister could accept the results: his Quebec caucus is very different from Trudeau's. Nonetheless, he gave his blessing to a complete reversal of the bargaining process. While the accord was designed to draw Quebec back into the constitutional fold, one that would be less harmful than the framework of 1982, Quebec was now running the risk of losing a great deal, if not everything.

The rules of the game that had been established in 1986 (settle the question of Quebec and deal with the rest afterwards) had now been set aside. Quebec was isolated, the fate of minorities and of those with insufficient legal powers.*

Five Weeks on a Roller Coaster**

The last three months of the constitutional saga would confirm, infirm, and then corroborate this analysis.

The House of Commons committee chaired by Jean Charest tabled its report on May 17, 1990. As expected, it was

* These recent events confirm the analysis in Chapter 5 of the 1982 constitution.

** Section written for the English-language edition

a smorgasbord. The idea was to please the three dissident provinces without alienating Quebec. The Charest Report proposed that the three dissident provinces adopt the Meech Lake Accord as is before June 23, 1990. Afterwards, the eleven governments would adopt a new constitutional resolution including some twenty amendments. There was something for each dissident province.

It may have come as a surprise to some that the Charest Report would be simply a shopping list. Every major issue, from the definition of the type of veto applicable to Senate reform to the "certainty" issue surrounding adoption of the accompanying resolution, was referred to a future conference of the eleven heads of government. The important thing was to show that Ottawa was exercising leadership and that it had been able to obtain support of the three federal parties for the report.

For a few days, the federal government basked in the praise heaped on this little catalogue by anglophone and francophone commentators, who fell in the federal trap and displayed their superficiality. It didn't take a lot of brains to see right through it.

For one thing, the Charest Report satisfied neither Manitoba nor Newfoundland. And then, by giving the federal government the obligation of *promoting* linguistic duality in Quebec and by restoring its exclusive right to create new provinces, the report was proposing two major changes to the Meech Lake Accord. It also proposed to state specifically that the distinct society clause did not compromise in any way the Charter of Rights. No matter what federal officials said, the report was unacceptable for Quebec.

The Conservative government had given orders to the Quebec caucus to remain silent, which could only make life harder for Robert Bourassa. The premier, however, could still rely on a joint resolution of the National Assembly, supported by the Liberal Party and the Parti Québécois and adopted April 5, 1990, that ruled out any present or future amendment to the Meech Lake Accord. As early as the evening of May 17, the premier of Quebec rejected certain crucial clauses of the Charest Report. But the forced silence of the Quebec Tories could make him appear isolated in the eyes of English Canada. Once more, the spectre of dual legitimacy was in the background. At the end of the day, who was speaking for Quebec, Brian Mulroney or Robert Bourassa?

François Gérin, a Conservative Quebec MP, wanted to recover his freedom to speak out. He quit the caucus to sit as an independent in the House and denounce the Charest Report. But a lone backbencher does not count for very much. (Remember Louis Duclos?) Much more would be necessary to jolt the government and force it to backtrack.

One man could do this by himself: the most important minister from Quebec, a close friend of the prime minister, and an accredited nationalist. By resigning noisily from the cabinet and the party, on May 22, 1990, Lucien Bouchard instantly destroyed any hope of negotiations on the basis of the Charest Report. He was acclaimed by public opinion in Quebec, except for a few editorialists. Robert Bourassa was thus in a much stronger position. For Bouchard, the Meech Lake Accord was now just one step on the way to sovereignty-association.

It was the end of the Charest Report. Everyone was back to square one. Brian Mulroney could no longer afford to stray from the Quebec government's position, knowing that his political future was bound directly to the Meech Lake Accord. Everyone wanted a last-chance conference. However, failure seemed very likely because of the distance separating Quebec from Manitoba and Newfoundland. (Frank McKenna's dissidence was now only tactical, and he had become part of Ottawa's strategy to bring the other dissidents into line.)

Bouchard's resignation shook up foreign exchange and bond markets. Foreign investors pricked up their ears. Instead of trying to calm them, the Mulroney government found new arguments in the situation. Perhaps the resignation would serve Mulroney's purposes. To intensify pressure on the dissidents, he raised, in concert with big business and the CBC, the spectre of Canada's breakup in the wake of the Meech Lake Accord's failure, which wasn't reassuring for the markets. He also delayed calling the premiers together, which he admitted in an interview with *The Globe and Mail*, excerpts from which were published June 12, 1990, three days after the Conference of the Last Chance.

The conference finally got under way on June 3. And the Canadian public witnessed something unheard-of in contemporary democracies: eleven men meeting behind closed doors from June 3 to June 9, coming out late every evening to feed generalities to a mob of journalists. New Brunswick having rallied behind the majority, as agreed, the last two recalcitrant premiers were subjected to considerable pressure by the nine other participants: "Do you want to go down in history as the gravediggers of Canada?"

Quebec was ready to sign an agreement to get discussion on Senate reform under way quickly, but refused to accept any amendment that reduced the relative number of senators from Quebec, and, even more adamantly, any attempt to whittle down the veto awarded by the Meech Lake Accord. Quebec also accepted, under certain conditions, a subsequent enlargement of the definition of Canada's fundamental characteristics to include native peoples and multiculturalism, in addition to the linguistic duality and the distinctiveness of Quebec society. Manitoba was very eager to obtain this "Canada clause," as well as Senate reform and the primacy of the Charter of Rights over the distinct society clause. The last two points were also part of Newfoundland's bedrock demands.

Quebec's commitment was a very small prize for Gary Filmon and Clyde Wells. They knew only too well that there is a big difference between a premier's signature and an actual constitutional amendment. Only the relentless psychological pressure, along with a surprising concession from the premier of Ontario, could get them to sign. David Peterson had a wild card ready to play: he was willing to give up six of Ontario's Senate seats in favour of the smaller provinces with the fewest, should comprehensive Senate reform eventually prove impossible to attain.

There was a great deal of wheeling and dealing, in which Jean Chrétien, the leader-to-be of the Liberal Party, took an active part. In the end, Gary Filmon, Sharon Carstairs, and Gary Doer finally accepted Meech II, which completed Meech I with an accompanying resolution. It included a few innocuous constitutional amendments and the broad outline of the negotiations that would begin immediately after June 23, 1990. However, the three Manitobans insisted on the necessity of holding public hearings in their province before putting the constitutional resolution to a vote. It took the form of an asterisk at the end of Filmon's signature.

Clyde Wells, premier of Canada's poorest province, refused to kneel completely. All he signed was a promise to submit the final package to a vote in the House of Assembly (or to a referendum) before June 23. The vote would be a free one. It was a second asterisk.

The two asterisks had no influence on the immense sigh of relief in the national capital during the night of June 10, 1990. But they gave the accord's opponents something to hang on to...and they prolonged the suspense until June 22. Native people were particularly upset that their concerns were pushed aside until the next round of constitutional bargaining. But what could they do?

Less than seventy-two hours after the signing ceremony, the accord was once more in trouble. Rules of procedure in the Manitoba legislature made it possible for any member to stall the whole ratification process. Gary Filmon had repeatedly warned that he needed at least four weeks to go through the various stages stipulated in the law of Manitoba. He was given only thirteen days! But who would risk aborting the accord? The answer wasn't long in coming.

Elijah Harper, an Amerindian member of the House, egged on by the profound dissatisfaction of his people and by public opinion in Manitoba, stalled debate day by day so that the constitutional paper died on the legislature's agenda June 22. Seeing that, Clyde Wells decided not to submit the resolution to his own legislature. He was not sure that it would go through, having personally continued to denounce the misdeeds of the accord right up to the last minute. He was also irritated by the pressure tactics of the federal government, which pretended that the legal deadline could be extended beyond June 23 if, and only if, Newfoundland agreed to pass the accord.

The constitutional saga was ending in acrimony, and the supporters of the accord had a scapegoat who was not aboriginal.

Once again legal considerations overshadowed the fundamental political issue. It was legally possible for Gary Filmon to suspend normal procedural rules with a simple majority vote in the legislature. However, he would probably have been defeated in the House on this question. Similarly, those who were indignant after Clyde Wells failed to follow through on his signature of June 9 apparently failed to grasp, first, that ratification of the accord by Newfoundland was by no means certain, and, second, that postponing the deadline hardly guaranteed a positive vote in the Manitoba legislature, given the fact that opposition was gathering steam, reinforced by the prime minister's own words that he had "rolled the dice" after delaying the federal-provincial conference as long as he could.

Quebec's threats, amplified by the federal government, were not taken seriously by most opponents of the accord, while others were eager for Quebec to make good on them. Right to the end, Pierre Trudeau waged his personal campaign against the accord, advising Clyde Wells and congratulating the native peoples. It did not make life any easier for

Jean Chrétien, who took over the Liberal Party leadership in the worst possible circumstances. Quebec nationalists were not saddened by the turn of events.

Looking Failure in the Eye

The failure of the Meech Lake Accord is the failure of a system, not of individuals. It is not Quebec that was rejected but the vision of Canada, a diluted one at that, which it proposed. English Canada refused to allow Quebec more latitude within Confederation. For twenty-five years, Quebec deluded itself into thinking there was a *third way* between federalism as practised and sovereignty, which it feared.

Quebec now realizes that the third way, even thoroughly laundered, provokes more and more resentment, recrimination, and existential doubt in the rest of the country. Quebec's minimum requirements are beyond the maximum that English Canada is ready to concede. In the meantime, the rules of the game within the present structure remain unacceptable to Quebec. The Mulroney-Bourassa alliance, symbol of Quebec Power, has come up against Canadian reality.

Canada is within its rights, but it cannot deny Quebec's right to draw the proper conclusions. On the evening of June 23 1990, Quebec was not at the same point it was on April 17, 1982, when the new constitution was given royal sanction. It will be impossible to behave as though the Meech Lake Accord had never existed. A totally new process is now under way.

The idea of two nations, which could not be introduced through the back door, will have to be dressed up for its arrival through the main entrance. But will it be possible to avoid a clash between the two nations? Can it be avoided even within Quebec?

CHAPTER 7

The Two Solitudes, Again and Ever

Hugh MacLennan found the perfect expression to describe the relations between French and English Quebecers: "Two Solitudes." It is the title of his second novel, published in 1945, which made his reputation. The expression has survived to this day and is now applied to the relations between Quebec and English Canada. But it is still applicable to the Quebec scene itself, where, after forty-five years, things have not changed that much between the two language communities.

The Marriage of Convenience

Quebec's ties to Canada are primarily determined by economic necessities. But even Quebecers with a gut feeling for Canada have a different conception than the one that moves English Canadians.

The vast majority of Quebecers are not in the least interested in the culture of the other Canada. Literature, television, cinema, it is all greeted with supreme indifference by French Quebec. The evidence is everywhere. Two or three will suffice. One of the best-known writers in English Canada is Robertson Davies. His stature is equivalent to that of

Michel Tournier in France or Gabrielle Roy in Quebec. Yet only two or three of his novels are available in French, and his name means nothing to Quebecers.

No television program produced in English Canada has ever been a hit with the public in Quebec, with the exception of a few miniseries (such as "Democracy"). The total lack of interest in the CBC's "Newsworld," broadcast for a few months solely in English Canada, is particularly significant. Surveys commissioned by Vidéotron, one of the two cable companies finally agreeing to carry the program in Quebec, show that Quebecers were not disposed to pay for it, not even ten cents a month. Few commentators have criticized the temporary absence of this service.

Lack of interest exists among all classes, including intellectuals. The cultural output of the Montreal anglophone community is also ignored. Hugh MacLennan's celebrated novel was translated into French a long time after its initial publication. Only Mordecai Richler seems to have escaped the general fate, perhaps because two of his novels have been brought to the screen. Few would know the answer if a sample of Quebecers were to be asked: "What artist born and living in Quebec is best known throughout the world?" It is neither Robert Charlebois nor Diane Dufresne, but Leonard Cohen, a real Montrealer and a great author, composer, and performer.

Demand is an important measure of the interest displayed for any given culture. But there are others. The people's contribution to an understanding of their country is also indicative of their interest for it. As it happens, Quebec's contribution to an understanding of Canada is about nil, as is its consumption of Canadian culture. There is not a single Quebec book on the general history of Canada,[1] and specialists in any facet of Canadian affairs are few and far between. Quebec economists and sociologists show more interest in the workings of Quebec society than of English-Canadian society. The same is true of English-Canadians' interest in Quebec.

But we should pause to dispel any possible misunderstanding. These observations are not in the least intended as accusations. It is not a question of ethnocentricity or "linguicentricity." Quebecers consume other cultural products than local ones. French and American works are also very popular. Time being a scarce commodity, Quebecers sampling cultural products from elsewhere will spontaneously choose whatever "speaks" to them most directly.

Canada, obviously, is not part of that universe, no more than Quebec is part of English Canada's, except for those artificial centres for French-Canadian studies. Why should it be otherwise? Why should a person from Toronto prefer Hubert Aquin to Marguerite Yourcenar, to mention only dead authors? It is not via Quebec that English-Canadians have access to "universal" values, to use a much-abused word. The converse is also true.

In spite of this fundamental cultural cleavage, almost as wide as the one dividing the French from the British, there are still people who are prepared for any verbal contortion in order to avoid saying or writing that Canada is made up of two nations. It is no tribute to their intelligence. But what is the point of discussing anything with people who claim the earth is flat?

It is perfectly logical for English-Canadians to show little interest in Quebec culture. Their southern neighbour is huge — and intrusive. This attitude is also perfectly logical for Quebec anglophones.

The English Ghetto

The fact that the two communities do not know each other at all, even in Montreal, enables pressure groups to impose a view of their community that conforms to their interests but not necessarily to reality. Imagine the Société St-Jean Baptiste acknowledging that some Quebecers are xenophobic. Imagine Alliance Quebec admitting that the majority of Quebec anglophones reject out of hand the idea of an essentially French Quebec and that this prospect disturbs them no end. No president of Alliance Quebec could ever be so candid; he would soon be dismissed from his post. It is not a question of persons but of the logic of institutions.

But after hearing and reading the same things over and over again, one ends up willy-nilly being converted (whence the importance of control of the news media for all authoritarian regimes). What makes it more likely is innumeracy, which is more widespread than illiteracy. When one can hardly calculate percentages and compare fractions, one loses sight of all the quantitative nuances inherent in social reality.

To speak of Anglo-Quebecers is to speak essentially of the Anglo-Montrealers who make up three-quarters of them. They constitute a real society, which is not the case with anglophones outside Montreal. The relations between the two are like those existing between Quebecers and francophones outside Quebec (Acadia being again an exception).

According to *The Gazette* and Alliance Quebec, Anglo-Montreal society accepts the new reality of Quebec. Well, not all its members, but almost. Most of those who refused to accept it left during the great exodus of 1977–79. The decisive criterion is a knowledge of French. The claim is that almost all young anglophones know French, and the proof is supposed to be found in the 1986 census, which shows that Quebec anglophones are now bilingual in a proportion of 58 percent.[2]

Let's have a look at this. The first thing is to arrive at a correct interpretation of the data. The question relating to linguistic ability reads as follows: "Can you speak English or French well enough to conduct a conversation?" (question 19 of the 1986 census). And that's it. What kind of conversation? At what speed? We don't know. This is a minimal criterion, and it is easy to imagine that someone who speaks French haltingly might answer the question affirmatively.

In 1986, 42 percent of Anglo-Quebecers and 45 percent of Anglo-Montrealers answered no to this minimal question. The media focused on the 58 percent who said yes, but, from the point of view of Quebecers, it is the 45 percent who said no that raise a few eyebrows. Granted that part of them are in Montreal for a limited time, but there is a large number who have been here for twenty, thirty, fifty years or more and who are incapable of shopping or ordering a meal in French, not to mention listening to a radio program. Two conclusions are possible: on the one hand, they never felt the *need* to learn French, given their demographic weight in the Montreal area, and, on the other hand, they were never *interested* in learning French.

The historical context explains a great deal, but one cannot read in the census data a high level of interest for francophone culture and lifestyle. This is reinforced by other observations.

The New McGill?

We will introduce here some interesting facts about an institution with an enviable reputation: McGill University. Our information comes from people who know it well. McGill was not chosen at random: one might expect to find there people who are open to the world around them.

McGill students fall into three categories: anglophones from Quebec (37 percent), francophones from Quebec (23 percent), and Canadians from other provinces (32 percent). Less than 10 percent of the student body is from abroad. According to the administration, 65 percent of Quebec anglophone students are able to get along in French; in other words, they are able to understand French, though not necessarily speak it.

One can see that standards are quite minimal. The picture comes into focus when students are asked directly. According to them, the proportion who are able to express themselves in French is less than 50 percent, and they are not necessarily capable of writing French.

What does this mean? That only a minority of anglophone students from Quebec, after *fifteen* years of schooling, would be able to hold a job requiring acceptable French. This is in 1990, sixteen years after Bill 22.

It would also be interesting to know the number of professors able to express themselves in French. We know, in fact, that they are not all bilingual — far from it — and that the same is true of Concordia University. One might think: "Indeed, it is a very interesting question. If university professors are not bilingual, who is?" But trying to get an answer turns out to be a waste of time: the administration at McGill considers the question of no interest. In any case, we know that the rate of bilingualism varies considerably from one faculty to another.

McGill University is nevertheless more open to the French fact than it used to be, more so than the majority of its anglophone students from Quebec, who don't feel any obligation to master the rudiments of the French language.

Other examples could be mentioned. But what is the point? If McGill's case is not conclusive, which one would be?

It is absolutely normal that a significant number of jobs in the Montreal area do not require any knowledge of French. After all, there are more than 500,000 anglophones in the metropolitan area. What is not so normal is the persistent effort to convince everyone that a majority of Montreal anglophones are now francophile and eager to benefit from the bicultural ambience of Montreal — while francophones huddle together shivering, afraid of the outside world.

It's the world upside down. There is not a single day when English-language media are not telling francophones that they represent a tiny island in the vast North American expanse. How can anyone be interested in a culture and a people that are deemed to be so marginal? The answer is a simple one: Quebec anglophones, allowing for exceptions, are not interested in Quebec culture or in French culture more generally. Indifference is the general rule. Yet it is precisely their minority status that incites Quebecers to open up to *la francophonie*...as well as to America.

These differences in behaviour will be obvious to anyone keeping an eye on daily activities in Montreal. The public in downtown anglophone movie houses includes a large proportion of francophones, while few anglophones attend French movies. The same situation exists in bookstores, theatres, and variety shows. English-language radio stations are obliged to give French songs *5 percent* of air time, most of them likely to be broadcast during the night.

A person would not be wrong in concluding that Quebec anglophones read very few French-language newspapers and books and listen to very few French songs. This has been confirmed by an important survey conducted by the ministry of cultural affairs.[3]

It is in this context that one must look at one of Pierre Trudeau's most cherished ideas.

The Bridge That Never Was

According to Trudeau, a dynamic culture has no need of defensive measures. A flourishing Quebec culture would be able to attract people of all backgrounds and absorb new arrivals. In other words, diverse cultures compete against one another — and may the best one win!

It is obvious that cultures do compete in certain domains. Quebec songs compete against French and American ones. The same is true of cinema. But the competition exists only for francophones, who have a choice between various cultural expressions. The quality of Quebec culture does not explain the indifference displayed by anglophones. The cause has more to do with their geographical situation. For anglophones, the real competition is between Canadian and American culture, with Quebec culture being of no account whatever. The most convincing proof is that anglophone indifference extends to all francophone cultural products, whatever their country of origin. But who would dare say that French culture is inferior to Canadian culture, whatever criterion is used?

This idea of Trudeau's loses all substance as soon as the general context of cultural competition is taken into account. Even if Quebec had the best writers, film-makers, composers, and singers in the francophone world, it would change nothing in the geographical and demographic context of North America. And it would not make French any more attractive for immigrants than it is in Montreal at the present time.

It is necessary to say a word about protectionism. Canadian culture is supported and protected in the same way as Quebec culture, which enjoys encouragement from Radio-Canada, the National Film Board, the CRTC, the Canada Council. Yet no one ever heard Pierre Trudeau denouncing this type of protection when he was in power. Does dogma on one side of the Ottawa River become heresy on the other?

Let us come back to Quebec, and Montreal in particular. The situation just described is light years away from what many francophones and some anglophones hoped for. It was possible to believe (particularly outside the English-speaking community) that anglophones would seek to maximize the advantages of their situation: "Anglophones in Quebec are twice blessed. They enjoy the use of their language and culture without fear of losing them, and at the same time they live in Quebec, the only place in North America where they can benefit from the presence of two world languages and cultures."[4] Thus they could have eventually contributed to bridging Quebec and the rest of Canada. However, for one William Tetley and one Richard French, how many Gordon Atkinsons are there?* History will remember that, more than anyone else, they served the cause of disunity between the two founding nations.

* Anglophone cabinet ministers in the first and second Bourassa governments and an Equality Party member of the National Assembly; Richard French resigned over Bill 178. Gordon Atkinson does not speak French after thirty years in Quebec.

The exodus of 1977–79 was the first warning sign. Retrospectively, the lull that followed was more like a cease-fire than a peace treaty. Hostilities resumed in December 1988 with Bill 178. Some are raising the spectre of a renewed exodus. But English Quebec and Canada are seeing things from a faulty perspective.

Understandably, the exodus that followed the Parti Québécois's rise to power had negative results for the anglophone community. On the other hand, all things considered, its results were generally positive for francophones. It must be noted that the migration of anglophones continued after 1980 until at least 1986, although in smaller numbers. In this light, it is interesting that francophone control of Quebec's economy proceeded more rapidly between 1978 and 1987 than between 1961 and 1978, particularly in the key areas of manufacturing and finance. The proportion of jobs under French control rose from 47.1 percent in 1961 to 54.9 percent in 1978, and 60 percent in 1987.[5] One should discount the alarmist speeches of those days, which masked the true state of affairs, in which Bill 101 would open more room for francophones, without solving the language question in a definite manner.

The apparent language peace that characterized the first half of the eighties can be credited to the prospect of a Liberal return to power in Quebec. After the event, in December 1985, there was a very loose enforcement of the provisions of Bill 101 regulating commercial signs, under the pretext that several cases were before the courts. Many people were shocked, and quite rightly so. It is an objectionable contradiction to demand respect for the laws one supports and turn away when others are transgressed. Is there any sorrier spectacle, in a country claiming to live under democratic rather than arbitrary and discretionary rule, than a minister of justice failing to uphold the law? Yet this is what happened in Quebec in 1986 and 1987. The minister in question, Herbert Marx, was caught in a trap of his own making in the turmoil of December 1988.

Slowly but surely, the situation was deteriorating.

Linguistic tensions were exacerbated when Quebec became aware of the magnitude of its demographic problem.* The concentration of young allophones, the children of Bill 101, in certain French schools drew attention to the enormous challenge of integrating new arrivals in Quebec society. Since 1986, there has been a surge in immigration, but two-thirds of all immigrants do not understand French when they land. As there are two communities in Montreal ready to receive them, and since there is, even today, no obvious reason why a non-francophone would choose the French rather than the English community, integration in the French milieu requires a supplementary effort on the part of the community.

We know that if nothing changes in the linguistic choices of the immigrant population, current demographic trends suggest that the relative importance of francophones in Montreal will decline somewhat over the next twenty years.[6] There are a lot of ifs, but the fact remains that the turmoil experienced in 1968 and 1969, at the time of Bill 63, resulted from a similar problem.

Anticipation of the Supreme Court decision on the language of commercial signs in Quebec was just as high, if not more so, than for the unilateral repatriation of the constitution in 1981. Anglophones had all their hopes set on this decision, while francophones were determined to preserve the integrity of Bill 101 at all costs. There was psychodrama in the air. It seems likely that the Supreme

---

* In his book, *Moi, je m'en souviens,* Pierre Bourgault refuses to accept the reality of the demographic problem. His thinking on this issue is obviously superficial. A society where 15 percent of the people are elderly is in a very different situation from one with 25 percent. He is also surprisingly indifferent to the prospect of a relative French decline in Quebec. There is a bit of Trudeau in Bourgault, that is, an identical belief in the power of the will to overcome insurmountable obstacles.

Court delayed publication to avoid having it fall in the midst of an election campaign whose main issue was the Free Trade Agreement. The campaign could have become utterly uncontrollable.

The decision was rendered December 15, 1988. It wasn't evident at the time, but this was the day the Canadian fracture began.

What's in a Sign?

The Supreme Court ruled that the ban on other languages but French in commercial signs was contrary to the Charter of Rights and Freedoms. The Government of Quebec could either accept the decision or invoke the "notwithstanding" clause in the Charter of Rights to maintain the existing ban. After some hesitation, the government opted for the second solution. But it sought to soften the blow by allowing the use of other languages *inside* businesses with fewer than fifty employees, on condition that French be more prominent. This is the essence of Bill 178.

The language war started up again. Bill 178 was the fifth language law in twenty years, if one includes the language clauses in the constitution of 1982. Anglophone protests were even more vocal than for Bill 101. There was a feeling of having been betrayed by Robert Bourassa (the author of Bill 22), who had promised, during the 1985 election campaign, that bilingual commercial signs would be made legal again. For most anglophones, the issue became one of principle. Bill 178 was unacceptable period. Hence there was considerable pressure on anglophone members in the government to resign from cabinet with a bang. But Bill 178 would not disappear: this then meant quitting the Quebec political scene at the end of their mandate.

In English Canada, dismay soon gave way to anger. Bill 178 stiffened opposition to the Meech Lake Accord among those who already had doubts about it, and encouraged a large number of uncommitted people to join them. It was a catalyst for all the sources of discontent feeding resentment against Quebec. The anglophone community in Quebec did a lot to fan the flames.

It was a great deal of commotion for a single law. To understand its ramifications, the political context is more important than legal niceties. In the course of the debate, it was forgotten that Bill 178 was perfectly constitutional. The use of the "notwithstanding" clause provoked massive criticism across Canada. However, since other provinces had already invoked the "notwithstanding" clause without any visible reaction, it is difficult to believe that the problem lies there. "Notwithstanding" clause or not, English Canada does not accept Quebec's ban on the use of English in commercial signs.

With a few extremely rare exceptions, no one in the nine other provinces came to the defense of Quebec. Yet there are clauses in Bill 101 that went much further than Bill 178, and no one is trying to revive the old embers.

For example, any locality where anglophones constitute less than 50 percent of the population cannot be considered legally a bilingual municipality, that is, it is not obliged to provide services in English, although most municipalities do so willingly. (This distinction between the letter of the law and existing social realities completely escapes English Canada.) For example, all professionals must be able to do business in French, even if their clients are almost exclusively anglophone. Finally, all American and British immigrants in Quebec must enrol their children in French schools, unless they want to assume the costs of an unsubsidized private school. How can one accept all these restrictions, even while grumbling, and deny Quebec's right to regulate commercial signs?

Some will reply: to regulate, yes, but to ban, no. In fact, this sums up the decision of the Supreme Court. But the distinction is not perfectly logical. The Supreme Court says: Quebec may *impose* the use of French for commercial signs, and even the predominance of French, but it may not ban the use of another language, or rather it has not proved the necessity of a ban. It means the court recognizes that the freedom of shopkeepers is not absolute. (It is fitting to point out that Quebec was obliged to legislate to impose French for commercial signs, with Bill 22 in 1974: this simple fact showed the true strength of French in the so-called second French city in the world.)

French predominance in commercial signs is already a major restriction on advertising freedom, justified by the Supreme Court on the basis of the linguistic environment of French in Quebec. However, once one recognizes the need for protective measures, it is impossible to reject the recourse to a total ban *on a matter of principle.* On a scale ranging from absolute freedom to total interdiction, the court is closer to the second than to the first.

A plague on legal subtleties! Who has noticed that Bill 178 was more restrictive than Bill 101? The latter accepted total bilingualism, inside and outside, for establishments with fewer than five employees. It preserved the cosmopolitan character of commercial signs in Montreal, and *no one* complained. However, this judicious compromise was thrown overboard so that the extension of inside bilingualism might be more palatable. The result was a foregone conclusion: nobody accepted the half-baked compromise. Passed amid confusion and improvisation, Bill 178 was politically and legally shaky. The debate, however, focused on the principle of the law.

The Masks Removed

In those days of December 1988, many bridges were burnt. The minority of anglophones who enthusiastically accepted the new Quebec must have felt terribly isolated within their own community. Everyone was thrown back fifteen years. The modus vivendi, thought to be well accepted, suddenly fell apart. The gulf between the two solitudes was as deep as ever, and 1989 would make it possible to count those who had learned nothing and forgotten nothing. William Tetley gracefully accepted Bill 178. But who else?

Not a single anglophone editorialist pointed out that, for more than two centuries, commercial signs in the western part of the city and in the rest of English Quebec were solely in English, and that, in any event, the law would be reexamined in five years' time. Must History be only a compendium of great deeds and noble attitudes?

They had learned nothing — certainly not politics. From the point of view of strategy, the anglophone community was to show extraordinary incompetence. After going on a political rampage, it heightened its own isolation — and was proud of it!

Three anglophone ministers resigned from the cabinet in December 1988. There were tremors in their voices and frenetic applause from their supporters. Originally, they were supposed to be four. But the fourth man, John Ciaccia, was also a member of the Italian community, the most important ethnic community in Quebec. It sent a clear message to its political representative: it would not understand if he resigned on a secondary issue and put the Italian community at odds with the francophone community. So he stayed.

A first split had just taken place between anglophones and allophones, who could easily turn the anglophone withdrawal to their advantage. Many are called but few are chosen for the command posts of politics. This opening split could have serious repercussions on the anglophone community, but the English chose to be blind.

A community, that occupies a distinct territory and feels ignored by the party traditionally representing it will be tempted to launch its own party. The foundation of the Equality Party may appear logical.* However, the object of

* It is significant that even the name of the party does not translate very well into French. Parti égalitaire is not suitable, since the adjective refers to social objectives, which have little to do with the party. Canadian Party would have been suitable, while Parti canadien sounds all right.

politics is to promote certain ideas effectively. Yet, since English is the first tongue of only 10 percent of Quebec's population, the creation of an *English Party* doesn't make any strategic sense. It would have been better to think of a broader coalition, to establish bonds with other groups and build for the future.

On the contrary, the Equality Party's platform is an outright rejection of the past fifteen years. The first major plank is commercial signs: the party wants to legalize bilingual signs, without the compulsory prominence of French. Its members, however, would have preferred complete freedom with no obligatory French. Only the intervention of writer Jacques Renaud, who threatened to quit the party, swayed members into including French in their sign policy.

The second major plank is access to English schools. The party wants unrestricted freedom of choice, which is a return to the situation prevailing fifteen years ago.

The third major plank is the Meech Lake Accord. The Equality Party rejects the current draft and wants substantial revisions.

There is nothing irrational about these positions. But, politically, they show a dramatic misconception of contemporary Quebec. This is no accident: how can one know another community without mixing with it, reading its newspapers and literary works, and being acquainted with its history? The Equality Party is the legitimate child of the indifference the majority of English Quebecers feel towards French Quebec.

Before the elections of September 25, 1989, analysts on both sides of the language barrier mocked this little party, which, in their view, was not representative of the average anglophone. But voting results were a clear refutation, providing, of course, that they be interpreted correctly.

In ridings where it ran candidates, it received 65 percent of the anglophone vote,[7] in spite of its political inexperience. The Equality Party defeated a very competent opponent, William Cosgrove, in Westmount (of all places), and even managed to drive Joan Dougherty out of Jacques-Cartier, after first attempting to recruit her. That cleared the decks. The two Liberals elected in the West Island survived thanks to the francophone vote. Outside its anglophone strongholds, the Equality Party's support was negligable, even among ethnic voters.

The anglophone community therefore took revenge on Robert Bourassa by electing four members of the Equality Party to the National Assembly. To top it all, two of them hardly speak a word of French. This community, so proud of its past, who could have and might still participate in the development of the new Quebec, has reduced itself to the level of a small ethnic community huddling against the cold.

They have consequently repudiated anglophones who want to participate in the life of Quebec, some of whom even organized in support of the Meech Lake Accord. Yet Quebecers, a quiet people, were not asking very much. Quebecers tend to forget how much they had to struggle to make sure their skating rink coincides with the territory called Quebec, the only one that history has finally left them.

A political analyst wrote somewhere, after the election, that anglophones had taught Robert Bourassa a good lesson. It would be difficult, with respect to history in the making, to be so far off the mark. The truth is that, on September 25, 1989, anglophones started sawing away at the branch on which they were so comfortably perched.

The Legendary Sheep

The various language laws of Quebec are often interpreted in English Canada as manifestations of a pushy and thin-skinned people. It is a serious error in perspective, just like seeing all of France in the curt reply of a Parisian waiter.

These laws are the product of age-old timidity. Timid people tend to fall back within the family circle and do not allow others to join them, particularly if those others do not share the same faith. And they say: "There are other schools than this one, they are English, but you can go there." It was realized, belatedly, what a foolish mistake this was. It became urgent to make up for lost time.

At that point, insults started raining down.

People politely raised their hands: "Would you be kind enough to print your menus in both languages? After all, many francophones eat here. Would you also be kind enough to put up signs in both languages? This is, after all, the second-largest French city in the world. No? Well, what we need is a law."

Insults began raining down again.

"So we will pass a law, a real one with teeth." And the whole country was terribly upset.

Nowadays, anyone following current events in Europe can observe that no Western nation is subjected to as many insults as the Quebec nation. Ethnic minorities, perhaps, but not a nation on its own territory. Daily, the descendants of those who put an end to the French-Canadian dream insult them in various Canadian media. True, only a minority behaves this way, but the majority does not seem to mind. Quebecers react inwardly, on the telephone when called for public opinion polls, or by writing letters to the editor.

Sun Life continues to do business in Quebec. And many francophones immediately switch to English, even when someone makes the effort to address them in their own language.

This is why language laws are necessary. If Quebecers had the same linguistic behaviour as the Flemish in Belgium (not necessarily a model, but offering an interesting parallel), anglophones would have become bilingual a long time ago (the ones who would have stayed, of course). A strategy of francophone penetration of the West Island, for example, would be perfectly conceivable at the present time; there is in these neighbourhoods a shortage of French schools and colleges. But no one wants to rush things; better let time do its work.

Such an attitude is defensible. But it does not prevent anglophone media from playing the same old tired song week after week: "Are we English welcome in Quebec?" and fuelling hostility everywhere in English Canada. The alliance between English Canada and Quebec anglophones, while it is not unnatural, complicates the Canadian problem instead of contributing to its solution.

If Quebecers rejected the anglophones, would they be so surprised at their indifference towards the world about them? Indeed, unilingualism is not the problem so much as the English community's systematic opposition to the claims of Quebec during the past twenty-five years.

However, the Quebec fudge is now hardening. A new generation of Quebecers, knowing how to count, willing to call a spade a spade, refusing to have the wool pulled over their eyes, is now in business. At the end of 1989, it was ready to step forward.

"Poor Quebecers who are wasting so much time over parochial matters..." These poor Quebecers, as it happens, would soon be feeling the wind of History in their sails.

It was a wind blowing from the East, and it would soon change into a hurricane. On the night of November 9, 1989, a new world was born. The Berlin Wall had come down.

CHAPTER 8

The European Spring of 1989

A certain idea of supranationality, alive for a long time in Quebec, was relegated to the attic by the revolution of 1989.

The night of November 9, 1989, when the Berlin Wall was transformed into a site of rejoicing, marks the end of an era and the beginning of another. The final disappearance of the wall was no longer in doubt after the massive exodus of young Germans from East to West Germany, by roundabout ways through Hungary and Prague. The exodus itself was inevitable after the removal of the Iron Curtain between Hungary and Austria. And so was this removal after the Hungarian regime's conversion to democracy. What we see at work in the East is a new and powerful momentum, the momentum of freedom.

Until October 1989, the big powers thought they might be able to control it. But November 1989 showed, to everyone's amazement, that a tidal wave will not be contained. The process launched by Mikhail Gorbachev, the inspired sorcerer's apprentice, has escaped him. *Twenty* days separate the opening of the Berlin Wall from the surrender of the Czechoslovak Communist Party.

Why this succesion of earthquakes?

The Revenge of Nations

In 1945, the two Europes, the American and Soviet ones, were in ruins. Food and coal were lacking. The world also discovered, as if what it knew already was not enough, that there was worse: there was Auschwitz and Birkenau, Mauthausen and Treblinka, and all the other camps.

Where was hope in 1945 and 1946? It was in the East. People were about to destroy the old world and give power to the oppressed, the working class. It was the end of personal dictatorships, bourgeois democracy, and national particularisms. Class against class, this was the course of history. Many people in Western Europe agreed. But those who knew Soviet history were grieving.

The rest is well known. Almost all of the nation-states of Western Europe recovered and prospered beyond expectations, while the people of Eastern Europe had to live by the Soviet model and see the disappearance of national independence. The model being mediocre, so were the results, making Soviet dictatorship even more unbearable. It weighed heavily on all important aspects of social life. For forty years, being in power in Eastern Europe (except for Romania) meant for all essential questions being a Soviet lackey.

It is not surprising, under these conditions, that the desire for *national independence* was the moving force in all serious protests, that being the prerequisite for any durable social reform and the cause of all visible and less visible Soviet interference. The Solidarity movement in Poland, from the very beginning in August 1980, was a movement of national liberation active in all sectors of society. Its ultimate goal was to take power so as to change the regime and realize Poland's independence, even though this was unmentionable at the time. Hope had long since changed sides. But the West would never move against the Soviet Union inside its sphere of influence.

This analysis, based on the permanence of national sentiment, could not anticipate the moment when these objectives might be achieved. It suggested, however, that the day these nations recovered their freedom existing governments would be swept away. But would the day ever come?

The answer was in Moscow.

When, on March 11, 1985, Mikhail Gorbachev became first secretary of the Soviet Communist Party, he had to confront an unwieldy economic system with substandard production. Military spending was eating up 15 percent of total resources (compared with 6.5 percent in the United States) and was accorded priority over production of consumer goods, as Soviet citizens knew only too well.

But the required *perestroika,* or restructuring of the economy, presupposed that the Soviet people would be informed of the gravity of the economic crisis; hence the need for *glasnost,* or transparence. For the Party, *glasnost* meant a more realistic interpretation of popular concerns. The most appropriate way of going about it was to hold elections where the people would choose among several candidates, with the victors meeting in a legislature endowed with real powers. Such were the principal decisions of a special conference of the Communist Party in June 1988. It was also a way of taking notice of the extraordinary excitement that a new sense of freedom encouraged throughout the country.

One can see that political democracy and economic restructuring could not but march together. Obviously, the party controlled the whole process and could not lose the semi-democratic elections of March 26, 1989. But the elections allowed Gorbachev's team to eliminate many of the supporters of the old regime. And, most important of all, they pushed the Party and the country along the road to democracy.

Another aspect of the new Soviet policy is worth mentioning here. The economic crisis demanded, and still does, a sizable cut in military expenditures. Hence the spectacular Soviet moves on disarmament. But it takes two to tango, so the Soviets had to convince the West of their peaceful intentions.

For the people of Eastern Europe, it was an incredible break. Yet there were two other factors. The first was that the Soviets realized that the benefits of economic control over Eastern Europe had been transformed over time into a net loss. Incredible as it may seem, exchange accounts within the Soviet bloc were based on barter. The Soviet Union was trading natural resources (petroleum and natural gas, particularly), easily sold on international markets, for industrial products of poor quality. It is to the advantage of the Soviet Union, therefore, to have exchange accounts founded on world prices. But for this to happen, the countries of Eastern Europe had to experience their own *perestroika*, and, of course, their own democratization.

The second factor had to do with the economic problems of Poland and, to a lesser extent, of Hungary. These two countries were counting on Western aid to pull them out of trouble. But the aid would be forthcoming only in a climate of democratization.

The march towards democracy was suddenly transformed into a mad dash taking everyone by surprise. Why? Because Moscow could not have it both ways: allow democracy to flourish, and control the process. The race towards democracy speeded up. In the eight months after the Soviet election of March 1989, Poland, Hungary, East Germany, and Czechoslovakia all experienced a change in government and announced a change of regime. It was the first peaceful revolution in modern history whose dual objective was democracy and national independence.

On the periphery, two other countries, Romania and Bulgaria, followed the general movement towards democracy. However, several hundred Romanians paid with their lives for the overthrow of Nicolae Ceausescu.

The dynamics of freedom had scored a home run with bases loaded. But it was only the beginning.

The New Europe

By underestimating the importance of national sentiment and the extent of communist economic inefficiency, many observers were wrong about the geopolitical consequences of the new course of events.* Nevertheless, there are now only a few nostalgic holdouts of the Cold War whose credibility is on a par with the ruble.

The opening of the Berlin Wall led directly to a reunified Germany.[1] Just a few weeks of freedom were necessary to refute the claims of East German intellectuals that the population was against reunification and preferred finding a "third way" between socialism and Western capitalism. After forty years of "cultural revolution," the idea of experimentation had soured. East Germans could also judge for themselves the capitalist misery of West Germany (in fact, they all used to watch West German television). Far from abating, the exodus of skilled workers accelerated.

A simple fact can demonstrate the artificiality of East Germany in the eyes of its own citizens. The campaign leading up to the election of March 18, 1990, was led from beginning to end by political parties from the other Germany. The only people the East Germans wanted to hear were Willy Brandt and Helmut Kohl, Christian Democrat chancellor of the Federal Republic of Germany. Victory was assured for his conservative allies after he rudely pushed aside the head of the Bundesbank (the central bank), promising the East Germans parity between the Deutschemark and their own Ostmark, plus rapid reunification.

"It will be too expensive, the Europeans must be reassured, and the Soviets, etc..." Reality turned out to be very simple; no one could oppose reunification if it resulted from a democratic vote. Helmut Kohl understood the profound resonance of the heartfelt cry, "*Deutschland einig Vaterland*"

---

* Two exceptions are worthy of mention: Jerry F. Hough, sovietologist at Duke University, and Zbigniew Brzezinski, President Jimmy Carter's foreign policy adviser.

(Germany, a single Fatherland). What did legal quibbles matter? Helmut Kohl presented foreign powers with a *fait accompli*, while reassuring interested parties with commitments costing little or nothing. This is a lesson in politics and statecraft!

Nothing could stop the march of reunification. Monetary and economic union came about on July 1, 1990, as a prelude to political union. The scheduled West German election of December 2, 1990, has been replaced by an all-German election. It is taking place less than thirteen months after the opening of the Berlin Wall!*

And NATO? And the Warsaw Pact? We're coming to that.

East Germany solved its problem by scuttling itself. Poland, Czechoslovakia, and Hungary have also only one thing in mind: to link up with the West as quickly as possible. There lies the future. The Soviet military presence on their territory is not wanted, to say the least. In the present context of détente, it was logical for these newly independent governments to request, politely but firmly, the withdrawal of Soviet troops (60,000 in Hungary, 70,000 in Czechoslovakia, 40,000 in Poland) and unilaterally cut back their own military spending.

The Warsaw Pact, which once made many Europeans tremble with fear, is becoming a bridge players' club.

The bulk of Soviet troops in Eastern Europe are in East Germany: 380,000 military personnel with their hardware, this is no mere platoon. Helmut Kohl declared with a great deal of shrewdness: We will fuse the two Germanys, but don't worry, you can stay where you are, and the Americans, the British, and the others will stay too. It is an unusual situation: a NATO country with 380,000 Soviet troops on its territory!

The Soviets are making wry faces. But if they want the Americans to leave German soil, they shouldn't be worried.

---

* This paragraph has been added to the English edition.

The new Germany will impose on everybody a disarmament even more spectacular than what was under discussion in Vienna in the spring of 1990. In this undertaking, it will have the support of many small and medium-sized European countries, including the Eastern triad, eager to cash their peace dividend.

Let's jump to 1992. Germany will have 80 million people and be the second or third economic power in the world (the Soviet Union is *not* a world economic power). And it would accept the presence on its territory of more than half a million foreign troops, the result of current arms negotiations in Vienna? Let's be serious. They will all be asked politely to pack their gear. We tend to forget that Allied soldiers are merely *tolerated* in West Germany.

And NATO? The principle of collective defense on which NATO is founded does not depend on the presence of Allied troops in Germany. It depends on an American nuclear guarantee in the event of a massive invasion by the Warsaw Pact. But one senses these concepts becoming more unreal from day to day. When Soviet troops have left Eastern Europe, when these countries have made their own security arrangements with their Western neighbours, it will then be necessary to find some extraterrestrial threat to prevent military specialists from dying of boredom. Is there a single specialist today looking into the parameters of a German attack on France?

The *Financial Times* of London reported on March 26, 1990, that Helmut Kohl was already proposing a new round of European disarmament negotiations, bearing mainly on... the presence of foreign troops on German soil. It is true that Margaret Thatcher is against it. But it is equally true that the Iron Lady has become the Glass Lady and that Helmut Kohl, the clumsy oaf, is in excellent shape.

Meanwhile, the Soviet Union is moving towards democracy and some form of market economy. There are many pitfalls along the way and unfolding events are being followed with bated breath. Yet the political significance of this change of direction is quite clear: the Soviet Union is crumbling under the weight of internal problems and desperately needs the West.

A Europe of Nations

What do we learn from this sidetrip to the Old World? Many things that concern us. Nations are still very much alive and continue making history and even shaking the columns of the temple. They are not melting away into supranational organizations represented a short while ago as the way of the future. Nations were thought to be obsolete: instead they still arouse emotion and enthusiasm. Today, they are even wrestling the last Empire to the ground. Anyone telling Lithuania, "Yes, you stem from an old civilization and you are a nation, but geopolitics is against you. So be reasonable and accept what your masters are ready to offer. With us, it's different, of course..." understands nothing about the times.

Some will point to the Common Market, the Europe of 1992, and, why not, the future European federation. Unification and integration, these are the tides of History! This type of statement is too often heard in Canada and warrants some answer.

We have seen that neither NATO nor the Warsaw Pact are in control of events. They have a hard time keeping up. There is a German interest, a Hungarian interest, a British interest, and so on. If they converge, all is well. If they diverge, discussions are necessary. But the United Kingdom cannot impose its will on West Germany, or vice versa. It can't tell Denmark what to do, and neither can NATO. The play of alliances is constant and changing. If NATO exists, it is because there is a common denominator. As soon as that is no longer present, NATO will cease to be.

The same is true of the European Economic Community, usually referred to as the Common Market. If there is a difference, it is more quantitative than qualitative. What national governments can do for their regions, by way of imposing a policy or an investment, the Common Market cannot do for even the smallest member of the club. At least not yet.

Europe is a grand and beautiful idea, born out of the most beautiful idea of all, peace. After so many fratricidal wars, Europe had to set up means of cooperation, to show that it was possible to work together. There also was a common enemy: the Soviet Union.

The Coal and Steel Community was set up in the early 1950s. The idea of a common market took shape and was put into effect by the Treaty of Rome, in 1957. Six countries signed it: West Germany, France, Italy, the Netherlands, Belgium, and Luxembourg. In 1969, the customs union became reality: internal duties were eliminated and common duties were collected on goods originating outside the Common Market.

Each signatory thought it was a good deal. The loss of sovereignty incurred by joining a common market was outweighed by expected benefits for national firms and the right to question the commercial policies of other members. These benefits, when they materialize, also increase the leeway of each state within its borders.

Agricultural free trade, however, was rejected in favour of a common farm policy designed to avoid premature dislocation of rural life. The European Economic Community determines farm prices and quotas and looks after surpluses. The policy eats up half the common budget. It is a political issue touching the very heart of the Common Market: from the very beginning, West Germany has contributed more than it has received. In 1988, for example, its net contribution totalled US$7 billion,[2] which comes to $110 per person. France is a net beneficiary. Some years ago, the United Kingdom raised an uproar to improve the balance between the two columns. But Germany demonstrated its European solidarity and refrained from making waves.

A form of regional equalization was also introduced to help economically stagnant areas.

Eventually, six other countries were accepted in the club, during the seventies and the eighties: the United Kingdom, Ireland, Denmark, Greece, Spain, and Portugal. Whence the expression "the Europe of the Twelve." Norwegian voters rejected membership.

The Twelve still exercise complete independence in their social, industrial, military, foreign, and demographic policies. Margaret Thatcher is completely free to dismantle the welfare state (if British voters will let her), just as François Mitterrand is at liberty to expand it. There are divergent attitudes about South Africa, the United States, and the Soviet Union. And even if there is a common commercial policy, in conformity with the Treaty of Rome, there is still no European economic strategy thirty-three years later.[3]

It is quite ironic that Britain and France are refusing to pool their nuclear strike forces for the defense of Europe. Europeans obviously prefer the American guarantee.

Since 1979, there has been a European Monetary System (EMS), and nine of the Twelve are participants. They are committed, on a daily basis, to a fixed parity between their respective currencies, but still retain the right to devalue or revalue as need may arise. However West Germany's economic power confers a preponderant role on its monetary policy. When the Bundesbank raises interest rates, other countries prefer to follow suit rather than be forced into devaluation.

Until the fall of 1987, all decisions within the European Economic Community were unanimous. One can imagine the tough bargaining going on backstage.

The Common Market is therefore one-tenth supranationality and nine-tenths national sovereignty, which has not stood in the way of a community spirit. This is Europe's lesson: while each member remains sovereign, there is a greater measure of cooperation and consideration for the concerns of other members. But, in the midst of a storm, each may stick to its positions, waiting for others to make the first move.

Naturally, in matters of internal trade, unfair competition, and agriculture, the Twelve must yield to the regulatory authority of the European Community, with a right of appeal to the European Court of Justice, which has the last word. The Community translates unanimous decisions of the Twelve into regulations.

Our chapter on Canadian federalism brought out the importance of regulatory authority, independently of the fiscal resources involved. The European Economic Community is a case in point. Those who say that Canadian federalism is too decentralized, or that it is moving in a contradictory direction to Europe, should note that the Community's budget amounts to 2 percent of the total fiscal resources of its twelve members.

A Triumph of Marketing

There has been so much talk about "the Europe of 1992" that the average person must wonder what kind of magic lies behind the phrase, particularly as discussions on economic and monetary union are gathering steam.

But the average person will be surprised to learn that the free circulation of goods and services within the European Economic Community is no sure thing, even in 1990. Quality standards applicable to goods sold nationally, or the accreditation of companies offering services of various types, still constitute non-tariff trade barriers that the Treaty of Rome has not eliminated.

To do away with remaining trade barriers and create "the single market" where goods and people will move freely (that freedom is now ensured for capital), some three hundred new directives are required. They are being drafted by the European Commission in Brussels, whose members, appointed by participating governments, constitute the Community's executive body. In this context, the rule of unanimity seemed too unwieldy and was replaced by a new rule of qualified majority. These are the two main thrusts of the Single European Act, signed in February 1986 by the twelve member governments. The act provides for the consolidation of the Common Market, to be completed by December 31, 1992. The target is a unified market of 320 million consumers.

We may be enthusiastic, but without losing sight of two points. First, even before the events of 1989, there was considerable apprehension about the task of harmonizing twelve national sets of laws governing, for example, taxation systems, immigration, professional standards and industrial concentration. Few specialists thought the end of 1992 was a realistic deadline.

Second, the media flurry on the "Europe of 1992" has distracted attention from everything *not* formally included in the Single European Act. The list is long enough to cool those who expect national sovereignty to fade all over Europe: social policy, defense and foreign policy. On monetary policy, nothing has really changed and there are no hints of a common economic strategy.

It is precisely for this reason that European militants are on the offensive. In 1988, the Twelve asked Jacques Delors, chairman of the European Commission ("Mister Europe"), to bring the heads of the twelve central banks together and have them prepare a report on monetary union. The so-called Delors Report, released in April 1989, outlined three successive steps leading to economic and monetary union, that is, fixed parities for the twelve currencies and a single central bank. This was not the first time the prospect had been mentioned, and, this time round, the authors of the report had the elementary prudence not to set a definitive timetable.[4] The first step is to bring all twelve currencies into the EMS in the very near future. It is, of course, the easiest one.

There are important differences on the question of monetary union. We will make note of one in passing. The

Twelve are in fact living in a zone dominated by the Deutschemark, without exercising any control over German monetary policy. But, with monetary union, they will henceforth have some say. Understandably enough, West Germany is taking precautions. At the end of 1989, the German government was suddenly busy with other matters and refused to advance the date of the summit conference on monetary union originally scheduled for late 1990. Should the European Community embark on this road, it will be on German conditions.

But consolidation is clashing with the Community's expansion. Austria has already asked for admission, and five other countries — Norway, Sweden, Switzerland, Finland, and Iceland — are thinking it over. But this is more of an administrative rather than a purely political problem. The real issue is elsewhere.

There is a Trojan horse looming on the eastern boundaries of the European Economic Community.

The Trojan Horse

Where is Europe headed? No one knows. The revolution of 1989 has upset the Eurocrats in Brussels. They can only respond to events. If any one had told them, in October 1989, that the economic and monetary union of the two Germanys would be realized during the summer of 1990, they would have called for a doctor.

West Germany is bringing its poorer kid brother into the European club without asking for permission. And the kid brother will benefit from the agricultural and regional subsidies of the Community. Germany's net contribution to the European till will be sharply reduced. Moreover, the future cost of rehabilitating East Germany is probably underestimated. Its industrial plant is antiquated, and the environment has been ravaged. Everyone suspected as much, but all is now confirmed: all economic statistics in East European countries had been designed for propaganda and not for information.

Relations within the Community are bound to be perturbed. Squabbles over national contributions will surface again. But the malaise will spread beyond these shopkeepers' quarrels, although they are important. The revolution of 1989 will bring to light divergent geopolitical interests among members of the Community. Look at the map of Europe: Spain, the United Kingdom, and Germany are not facing in the same direction. Germans have lived for centuries in the eastern part of Europe, which is now inviting them to come in and to bring their capital and their technology.

Europe's centre of gravity will shift eastward, where 250 million people are demanding European status. Could one imagine a more indisputable victory for Western Europe? And when Czechoslovakia, Hungary, and Poland come knocking on the door, can they be turned away? Yet such an expansion in the size of the European Community is not compatible with its consolidation.

The motor of real European political integration will soon be idling. Yes, one hears a lot about it nowadays. He who peers behind the slogans will see how the timorous drape themselves in lofty words. Who, for instance, has proposed a true European government issued from and responsible before the European Parliament? The answer is: no one.

The Cold War helped sustain a certain European ideology. But the disintegration of military blocs means the end of the dream, not of the European Community or of European confederation, but of the United States of Europe. Greater economic integration does not necessarily lead to political unity. This is for the better: what else sets limits to economic power but political power?

There could be worse for Europe than a Trojan horse with a human face. Even if the European Community does not progress beyond "1992" and a form of monetary union, Greater Europe will still be the womb of the future.

Chapter 9

The Prince of Ambiguity and His Four Jokers

Just as an irresistible momentum is carrying the Old World forward, Canada is about to start the same process. The players are acting out their roles, spectators are either applauding or creating an uproar. The one difference from the theatre is that the players are hiding their scripts and don't know what lines the others will be speaking. By coming closer, one might be able to discern a vague sort of script.

At what point did English Canada cease wanting Quebec? Tomorrow's historians may argue the point. But we can't be mistaken if we point to 1989: after Bill 178 and before the explosion of anti-Quebec sentiment. Wasn't there something pathetic in the daily tally that placed Ontario municipalities in two parallel columns, one for those declaring themselves unilingual and another for those refusing to do so? And what about the failure to recognize that something had snapped in the country?

The furious outbursts against the French fact did not target any specific expenditure or service. They occurred where unilingualism was already in force. They did not change anything. But they sent a clear message to all francophones in the area and beyond that the crusade against bilingualism in all its forms had just been declared. And no one reacted: neither Queen's Park nor Ottawa came out waving a big stick. These municipalities had the support of a majority of ratepayers, and there were fears at other levels of government of provoking more ill-tempered moves. Public opinion in English Canada wavered between indifference and support for unilingualism.

By a quirk of fate, these events coincided with the agony of the Meech Lake Accord. The principal players in this drama, with strong support from home, were frozen in irreconcilable positions. One of their first preoccupations must be to pin the blame on someone else in a credible way. But what is there to fear? After June 23, 1990, who will ask, "Who lost Quebec?"

The Vigil

Quebecers noted all this, each in their own way. The Sault Ste. Marie syndrome had its effect, but the essential meaning of the failure of the Meech Lake Accord is also beginning to sink in. Only two options are left: the status quo, or a complete overhaul of the relations between the two nations. We have seen that Quebec cannot be satisfied with the status quo. It is not surprising, then, that public opinion in Quebec should have started shifting.

Certain signs might have been detected in public opinion polls in the fall of 1989, as well as in the pronouncements, rather favourable to sovereignty, by some diehard federalists such as Father Georges-Henri Lévesque, the Dominican who set up the department of social sciences at Laval University during the heady days of the anti-Duplessis struggle.

And then the new business establishment came in to save the accord from sinking. It was a replay of the last weeks of the free trade campaign in November 1988, when the rising stars of business did everything to sway public opinion in its favour. A committee for the Meech Lake Accord was organized and the pilgrim's rod was handed to a delegation of prominent Quebecers: the holdouts in English Canada had to be converted. But it was a wasted effort. A stick with no fuse is not very convincing.

However, businessmen are not politicians. Professionally, they think of solutions and scenarios. So, if the accord fails? Well, many replied, we'll pick up our marbles, we can go it alone. In other words: independence-association. Nothing to be afraid of. Orthodox federalists were bowled over. But not public opinion, which was already aboard the bandwagon. In December 1989, close to 60 percent of Quebecers were favourable to sovereignty-association in the event of the accord's failure,[1] that's two-thirds of the francophone population. The failure looked as though it would sway a large proportion of nationalist federalists, that is, conditional federalists.

Such interventions of businesspeople can only stimulate the historical rise of pro-sovereignty sentiment. In effect, it amounts to an economic endorsement of sovereignty, something that has always been lacking.

One must understand the forces at work. If Michel Gaucher, CEO of Steinberg, or Claude Béland, president of the Mouvement Desjardins, only spoke for themselves, their words would have only anecdotal value. But such is not the case: these two personalities reflect the views of most of the new Quebec establishment. *Had they been minority voices in the business community, they would not have spoken out.* It was the supporters of the status quo who were keeping silent during this vigil.

There is surely a tactical element in these veiled threats. The idea is to increase the pressure on the three recalcitrant provinces that reject the accord as it stands. But the strategy is rather curious. As a form of blackmail, the threat of independence will antagonize those to whom it is addressed and show that the speaker does not really consider himself part of Canada. Quebec misreads political sentiment in other provinces.

On the other hand, raising the ante makes it harder to pull back eventually. It is difficult to cover one's tracks when they are everywhere. Public opinion will remember. In any case, anyone familiar with the contents of the Meech Lake Accord knows it can never satisfy the thirst for autonomy that drives public opinion. For many Quebecers, it is not a question of choosing between the Meech Lake Accord and sovereignty but of having both. Quebecers are "*étapistes.*"*

Even though the new guard constitutes a "tightly-knit society," to use sociologist Marcel Rioux's phrase, this is not enough to explain their statements of confidence, whatever the political future, which contrast markedly from those of 1980. Under these statements, a hard rock is pushing out.

Red Ink

For a marriage of convenience to last, reason must find a certain satisfaction. In Quebec, the red maple-leaf flag pales next to the fleur-de-lis. Federalism must be profitable for a majority of Quebecers to rally behind it. The idea was played to the hilt during the No campaign in 1980. It no longer works in 1990.

The profitability of any political system is hard to assess. Many elements have to be weighed: the narrow balance sheet of the accountants, the access to a broader market, and the human and material cost of the overlapping jurisdictions that are characteristic of relations between Ottawa and Quebec and the resulting political inefficiency. The market opening is not in question and will be preserved whatever happens. The situation thus calls for a positive balance sheet to make up for the negative aspects of federalism, shown by the failure of the accord to be almost beyond reforming.

The balance sheet approach weights Ottawa's revenues from Quebec, mainly direct and indirect taxes, against cur-

---

* Etapism was the step-by-step approach to obtaining independence promoted by Claude Morin, intergovernmental affairs minister under René Lévesque.

rent expenditures in the province, including goods and services, and transfer payments to individuals, businesses, and the provincial government. The balance sheet is incomplete if one fails to include, during periods of deficit financing, Quebec's share of that deficit. The importance of this point will not escape anyone who has followed developments in Canadian public finances over the last fifteen years. If one fails to take the deficit into account, we face an absurd situation: the balance sheet for *every* province could show a surplus, since Ottawa can use deficit financing to spend more than it collects.

There are also methodological problems. The key one is probably how to calculate each province's financial contribution to the federal deficit. Some have recently suggested a demographic yardstick:[2] if Quebec represents 25.5 percent of the population, its contribution to the deficit will be of the same order. An economic yardstick seems more appropriate: Quebec's contribution to the national economy is about 23.5 percent. This criterion changes the balance sheet slightly, but the general tendency is the same.

There is a striking parallel between the growth of pro-independence sentiment and the profitability of the Canadian link. Data on the benefits of federalism are available only from 1961 to the present.[3] From 1961 to 1971, the balance sheet is clearly negative for Quebec. It is positive only after 1973, the year in which the Parti Québécois became the official Opposition in the National Assembly, with all the research credits and media coverage attached to this position. This favourable phase came to an end in 1986, as federal authorities began using every possible means to slow the growth of the national debt. The table shown here illustrates the consequences for Quebec.

The federal government thus had "surpluses" in Quebec for 1987 and 1988 of $700 million and $1,100 million. (That is, the deficit was disproportionately spent outside

Balance Sheet of Federalism for Quebec
(in millions of current dollars)

	1970	1975	1980	1985	1986	1987	1988
Federal current expenditures in Quebec	3,398	8,681	15,194	26,177	25,740	26,266	27,843
Federal revenues from Quebec	3,806	6,645	10,738	17,165	19,603	21,559	24,108
Balance	-408	2,036	4,456	9,012	6,137	4,707	3,735
Quebec's share of the federal deficit (23.5 percent of total)	—	752	2,463	7,305	5,640	5,381	4,815
Net balance	-408	1,284	1,993	1,707	497	- 674	-1,080

Sources: 1970-1986: Statistics Canada, Catalogue 13-213S, *Provincial Economic Accounts 1961-1986;* 1987-1988: Statistics Canada, Catalogue 13-213, *Provincial Economic Accounts, 1984-1988*; and Department of Finance, Canada, *Annual Reference Tables,* June 1989.

Quebec.) The trend is even more pronounced in the federal budgets for 1989 and 1990: taxes have been raised while transfer payments to the provinces have been cut.

In this context, one fundamental point must be made. It is understandable, in times of crisis, that all members of a federal system contribute to the relief of a severe budget squeeze in the national government. However, Quebec's contribution exceeds its real economic weight within the federal system. A few examples will do. "In 1980, 35 percent of federal business grants went to Quebec and 18 percent to Ontario. In 1988, Quebec was getting 17 percent and Ontario 23 percent."[4] In a more general way, during the 1980s, Ottawa's current expenses have increased much more rapidly in Ontario than in Quebec. National belt-tightening is easier on Ontario. Should one be surprised?

In 1990, the membership fee in the club of irrational federalism is more than $200 for *each* Quebecer, young or not so young. In exchange we have a ringside seat to view the guerilla war our two governments have been waging for forty-five years — and money for the ammunition is now coming right out of our pockets.

However, those who believe that Quebec Power has finally run out of steam in Ottawa are out of sync. By a year or two?

The Stone of Sisyphus?

There is certainly a great deal of irony in the fact that federalism becomes expensive for Quebec just when the government most sensitive to its aspirations is in power in Ottawa. The problem is structural: when the pie is shrinking, competition is fierce. Those with the sharpest elbows get more.

The present government, in power since September 1984, inherited from its predecessor a financial crisis of the first magnitude. The flow of red ink had been growing rapidly since 1982. In 1984, the budget deficit came to 6.8 percent of the national product. It is the worst performance among the seven leading Western powers after Italy, which is a special case because of the importance of its underground economy.*[5]

The dynamics of deficit accumulation are well known. Deficits are necessary during periods of recession to sustain economic activity. But if the public debt continues to rise sharply after the return of prosperity, deficits quickly turn into a serious problem. Interest payments take up an increasing share of public revenue, forcing the government to raise taxes and cut other expenditures. Should another recession hit the economy before the public debt is brought under control, it will skyrocket, precipitating a major financial crisis. From 1980 to 1990, federal debt has grown from $72 billion to $352 billion.

The pursuit of financial stability means Ottawa has only limited freedom of action, at the present time, for economic

* In *Towards a Just Society, The Trudeau Years,* published in March 1990, not a single paragraph, in fact not a single line, is devoted to the public debt *problem.*

and social policy. The situation is a handicap for Quebec and its businesses. Moreover, the rationality of the political system is further undermined.

Energetic deficit reduction is hampered by the difficulty of cutting back on the federal government's largest spending programs, transfer payments to individuals (old age benefits, unemployment insurance, family allowances). The Mulroney government got into hot water in 1985 when it attempted a partial deindexing of old age pensions. It barely managed a partial deindexing of family allowances. After the election of November 1988, it succeeded (the Senate willing, that is) in trimming the principle of universality in old age benefits and family allowances with the clawback provision. Only in the medium term will these steps have a visible effect on public spending.

Any attempt to reform the transfer payments program triggers strong protests among those affected. So why not tackle the deficit in a way less politically damaging, which is to cut back another big spending program: transfer payments to the *provinces?* This has been Michael Wilson's strategy in his last few budgets. The budget tabled in February 1990 shows black on white that, from 1990 to 1992, transfers to the provinces are almost frozen at the level of 1990 ($26 billion) while transfers to individuals will rise from $38.7 billion to $45.2 billion.[6]

The political rationale for this policy is self-evident. But let us look at one of its consequences. Part of the payments to the provinces is a federal contribution to health care programs, which will be reduced year by year. We are now familiar with the acute problems surfacing in health care: overcrowded emergency wards, shortages of hospital beds, interminable delays for certain types of surgical operations. People are dying as a result of these delays. The universality of health care is being severely tested while old age pensions continue to be paid in full to people with a net income of up to $50,000, people who also benefit from a lower tax burden than younger persons with an equivalent income!

So this is the system that keeps us in the vanguard of human progress, as the sycophants of Canadian federalism would have us believe?

Provincial governments may try to compensate for a shortfall in revenue by shifting the burden to local institutions such as municipalities and school boards. But it is easier said than done. Provincial governments are forced into more austere management. From 1985 to 1988, they have accumulated a combined deficit of $14.5 billion. And how about Ottawa? For roughly similar total expenditures, a $99-billion deficit.

To all appearances, it will be a while before federalism benefits Quebec once again. The first joker, the cost of federalism, is already in the wings.

The Prince of Ambiguity

On the eve of St-Jean-Baptiste Day in 1990, what will Quebecers think of the present federal system? Three words will do: unprofitable, irrational, and irreformable. The strategy of spreading Quebec's resources between two levels of government may have been worthwhile for a fairly long period, the time necessary for Quebec to modernize and develop its human resources. However, the eighties have shown the limits of this strategy. Quebec finds itself politically weak within the present system: its partners go so far as to deny it the name of nation. Moreover, Quebec is powerless to change the system from within. Who can be sure, in this context, that the future won't be a replay of the last twenty-five years? So?

So it is possible to do better. The strategy of dispersal can be replaced with the strategy of concentration. Ottawa does more than Quebec for Quebec culture, for scientific research, for the expansion of certain business sectors, and so on. Ottawa has a large budget and imposes its own agenda, which often contradicts Quebec's. Therefore, repatriating all these funds and human resources would do away with overlapping jurisdictions and allow people and businesses to operate in a more orderly context.

At the present time Quebec's sovereignty, even within its own jurisdiction, is quite narrow. On the other hand, Quebecers are minority participants in the government of Canada. It wouldn't be a bad idea, for linguistic, economic, and social reasons, to trade this participation, uninspiring for most Quebecers, for the type of political sovereignty similar to that of the smaller countries of the European Economic Community. On the contrary.

This trend of thought will be more prevalent with the approaching deadline of June 23, 1990. Other voices will be heard, warning Quebecers against the possibility of things getting out of hand, or saying that nothing fundamental has changed and that the constitutional jigsaw can be reconstructed with a bit of goodwill. Others will point to the dangers of economic instability arising out of the breakup of Canada.

All eyes will be on the premier of Quebec.

The most naive will expect Robert Bourassa to come out with a ringing endorsement of federalism *or* sovereignty. This simple judgement shows the character of the man who has juggled the two contradictory options for many years. Indeed, true federalists think the premier is a closet separatist, while diehard supporters of independence see him as a federalist whose only concern is hanging on to power. (The truth is more trite and yet more intriguing: Bourassa is the image of the majority in francophone Quebec who happen to be very conditional federalists.)

No, the premier will not make any grandiose statement with a hand on his heart. And Robert Bourassa does not like instability.

Yet, in the early summer of 1990, any premier of

Quebec will be standing at the focal point of Canadian politics *with all or almost all of the best cards in his hand.* He will be in a position to make history. Every person involved in politics has dreamed of such an opportunity. It would be surprising indeed if Robert Bourassa had not sized up the situation.

What cards does he hold? We saw that the economic card is changing hands. Out-and-out federalists are losing it: the burden of the proof as regards the benefits of federalism will fall upon them. Their best card has to be the fear of political instability and its consequences, which, one should note, does not seem to have alarmed opponents of the Meech Lake Accord.

But isn't the Liberal Party of Quebec federalist? Isn't that a major obstacle? Interpretations and analysis often go off the track on this point. It is a fundamental error to think that the turn of events is embarrassing for Premier Bourassa, that the Liberal Party is totally confused, or that the Parti Québécois is riding high.

The premier of Quebec heads a party that is now federalist and nationalist. Since his political comeback in 1983, he has never made Trudeau-style speeches against the *idea* of sovereignty. Instead, he has been harping on the economic instability it *might* bring about. It is true, Liberal ministers and members of the National Assembly are federalists, with only a few exceptions. There is even among them a group of diehards, made up of anglophones and a few francophones.

As soon as the Meech Lake Accord seemed likely to fail, Robert Bourassa's first concern was to test his party's state of mind. Hence the brief statements he made on a visit to West Germany, in February 1990, about the possibility of a new "superstructure." It is hard to understand why these probes were greeted with laughter here, since they actually set the groundwork for the post-Meech debate in Quebec and within the Liberal Party. The leaders of the new francophone establishment leapt into the debate and were soon joined by all of the conditional federalists in the Liberal Party.

During the general council meeting of the party, February 24 and 25, 1990, diehard federalists must have wondered if they hadn't strayed into the wrong conference room. The meeting had been called ostensibly to set up a study committee to determine available options in case the accord failed. Politically, it helped determine the party's feelings on this matter *and* prepare minds for a major policy shift. People became very talkative. Four months before the official demise of the Meech Lake Accord, about half the Liberal members of the National Assembly and an important proportion of the cabinet were having a close look at sovereignty-association.

The election of September 1989 not only demonstrated that the sovereignty option was in good health but also revealed that there were now a number of Liberal *souverainistes.* Public opinion polls over the winter of 1990 showed this group was growing all the time. What did it mean?

When language conflicts in Canada were linked to the constitutional gulf separating Quebec and English Canada, sovereignty began losing the sulfurous undertones it still carried for a great number of Quebecers. For them sovereignty has been identified with the Parti Québécois, and, for many economic and social reasons, they didn't like it. But what could be more reassuring than the Liberal Party? An expanding minority of Liberal voters were willing to give the party a blank cheque for a policy shift that was once unthinkable but will seem quite natural tomorrow.

The shift among Liberal voters has radically transformed the political momentum in Quebec. Sovereignty has become the choice of a growing *majority.* Liberals disappointed with federalism, in the feverish summer of 1990, will display a new spirit of activism and try to convert the party. The situation of francophones attached to federalism will become more difficult within the party. They will be trapped between public opinion polls and their own convictions, just like militant *souverainistes* in 1985, when the Parti Québécois turned neo-federalist. Is federalism worth the sacrifice of a political career? Anglophone Liberals will likely return home, very much alone.

Any commentator expecting the Liberal Party to be the scene of a fight to the end between federalism and sovereignty is being short-sighted, even though the two options stood about equal in March 1990. One is rising and the other falling.

Shouldn't a premier be governing in the name of the people? He will give the movement ambiguous encouragements. Public opinion polls, which are for the premier what the telescope is to the astronomer, will allow him to keep the lid on potential fracas and bolder allusions to his royal prerogatives. The Liberal Party will follow its leader...who will be following it.

The joker of public opinion is sewn to Robert Bourassa's vestpocket.

How About the Plumbing?

Such a shift implies that there is an alternative to the present federal system. Some think Quebec can just slam the door and live on its own without worrying about English Canada, once the assets and liabilities of the federal government have been split and the Quebec share of the public debt agreed upon. Just old-fashioned independence. The free trade pact between Canada and the United States has fostered illusions on that score.

Obviously, the free trade pact would continue to apply to Quebec, even after an independence is worked out with scissors. It would take a really bad turn of events before Canada would want to isolate Quebec economically. It would not be in its interest, given everything Quebec buys and could easily procure elsewhere: wheat, beef, industrial equipment, and so on. It is true, of course, that vexation and reason make poor bedfellows. But the fact is the mood of English Canada in 1990 inclines towards resignation rather than aggressiveness. Free trade with the United States will survive.

The illusion is in the belief that Quebec could easily replace the Canadian market with the American one. There is actually a greater degree of economic integration with the rest of Canada (and particularly Ontario) than with the United States. A few figures will illustrate this point: in 1987, Quebec's exports to the rest of Canada were greater than its exports to the United States, even though English Canada's economy is *thirteen* times smaller than that of the United States.[7] East-west integration is therefore stronger than north-south. The data contradict the idea that it would be easier for Quebec to trade with the United States than with Ontario.

However, the data also indicate the *growth* of exports to the south will be more easily achieved than to the west, given that Quebec's penetration of the American market is so much weaker. But Quebec needs continuing links with the Canadian economy to derive net benefits from larger export volumes to the United States.

The simplest way is to hang on to the Canadian dollar. There is a broad consensus on this question. A Quebec currency is an attractive idea and might even yield economic benefits in the medium term. But it is not practical politically: the costs of the transition might prove prohibitive, and such a step would go against current trends, particularly within the European Common Market.

There is sure to be, over the next few months, a great deal of debate in Quebec on the Delors Report. It proposes, for the next decade, the establishment of fixed parities for the twelve currencies and a central bank for the European Economic Community. The first goal has since been replaced with the idea of a common currency. It is doubtful that Europe will bring the project to completion, at least not in the near future. In any event, the real issue is not there. Within a few years, the twelve governments are likely to reach the second stage of setting small bands for the relative values of their currencies.

Two comments are in order here. The first is that no fundamental difference exists between a common currency and national currencies whose relative value is permanently set, or almost (for example, one mark being equal to 3.35 French francs). One advantage of a distinct currency is that its relative value can be changed so as to stimulate exports and inhibit imports. But a common currency has one advantage for a more dynamic country: the partners can't use devaluation to hold their own.

The second comment concerns Quebec directly. A common currency means a single central bank, hence a single monetary policy. Although it might be exaggeration to say "one currency, one budget," it is clear that two countries with a common currency cannot pursue conflicting budget policies for very long. There must be common budgetary rules, which set limits on national budget deficits. There is a great deal of discussion on this point in Europe.[8] It is a happy coincidence.

Quebec is currently penalized by federal fiscal policy, as we saw, and by high interest rates partly attributable to the size of the deficit. Common budget rules? Quebec would be ready to sign on the spot.

After these considerations, we can see the outline of an alternative for the federal system, for which supporters of the status quo will be clamouring. A common currency, a common market for goods, capital, and persons. The counterpart would be the devolution of all fiscal powers to the Quebec government and the end of the Canadian government's legislative authority on Quebec territory. The end of fragmented jurisdictions, in fact. Starting from this plan, it is possible to discuss pooling certain resources and coordinating certain policies.

It sounds very much like sovereignty-association. It could also be called the beginning of a new Canadian economic community. No doubt this sketchy outline will raise countless questions on all its aspects and on all the loose ends that are bound to show. But that would be putting the cart before the horse. When building a road, the first thing is to choose the destination and then one worries about the technical details...unless one feels that the road itself is impossible to build. But there are not many left in Quebec who think that way. Similarly, when the two Germanys agreed on reunification, they didn't say: "Let's make an attempt at monetary union, and if it works we will proceed further." Not at all. They agreed on principles and then turned to technical issues.

All plumbing problems will be resolved by plumbers, as they should be. We know already that a lot of paper will be shuffled from one side to the other and that many people, particularly in Ottawa and Hull, will find themselves in new offices. And that's about it. It's a lot and at the same time very little. The economic plumbing will stay in place. Why should the copper pipes be changed?

Let's call this the European joker.

But since when does a government show all its cards before negotiations begin?

The New Tories

Only profiteers believe that money buys everything. At least one staple is beyond the reach of money — time, which is *not* money. Who doesn't lament the passage of time? Who hasn't regretted wasting a unique opportunity or failing to appreciate an unusually favourable set of circumstances?

There are opportunities that must be seized under pain of turning into a historical footnote. Not all moments are propitious for launching a probe to Mars or Jupiter. There are windows of opportunity. Military historians know that numerous campaigns would have ended differently had some giant opening been put to use or some portent properly understood.

There are bureaucrats of politics and there are magicians of power. There are those who watch the parade and those who make history. There is Adélard Godbout* and there is Charles de Gaulle.

A unique opportunity is arising in the national capital, more particularly in the House of Commons. Since September 1984, there is a group of Quebec MPs who think "Quebec First": they see themselves as promoters of Quebec's interests rather than representatives of Canada in their own province. A large number of MPs and cabinet ministers would be ready, in the event of a major confrontation between Quebec and the rest of Canada, to support the government of Quebec. This is the fourth joker of the premier of Quebec.

This can naturally only be used if everyone stays in place. A string of resignations involving leading representatives of Quebec in Ottawa, in the wake of the Meech Lake Accord's failure, would be particularly inept. There will be a lot to do in Ottawa, inside or outside the main federal parties. Should Quebec proclaim its intention of reopening the compact of 1867, the presence of friends and allies in the House of Commons is absolutely indispensable for facilitating the ensuing negotiations. Of course, there will have to be mutual consultations between the Quebec government and the Quebec bloc in the House of Commons.

There are two things to remember. The first is that, on two occasions in recent parliamentary history, political parties have paralysed legislative operations to block government initiatives deemed to be illegitimate. In March 1981, the Conservative Party forced Pierre Trudeau to give up unilateral patriation of the Canadian constitution until he had obtained an opinion from the Supreme Court as to its legality. In 1989, the New Democratic opposition in Sas-

* Liberal premier of Quebec 1939–44. A good man, but very weak before the federal government.

katchewan forced Premier Grant Devine to withdraw a bill privatizing the publicly owned potash industry.

The second has to do with the relative strength of parties in the House of Commons. In March 1990, the Conservatives had a majority of forty seats. A shift involving twenty-one Conservative MPs could threaten the government's survival. How many Conservatives were elected in Quebec the last time around? Sixty-three. There is room to spare...

Four jokers in one hand is enough to take the pot. Of course, one must be ready to play them, just in case other players have not seen them.

Yes, but how? How to reach the epilogue without too many scratches and bitterness on both sides of the Ottawa River?

The last act is now beginning.

CHAPTER 10

The Quiet Resolution

Internal divisions are nothing new in Canada. The country has had its share of existential crises since 1867. They always concerned relations between the two nations. What is new, at the beginning of 1990, is the profound division within English Canada, where a minority is willing to take a modest step towards Quebec while the majority considers Quebec just another province, no more, no less. Once again, Quebec is dividing the country. It is not Brian Mulroney, as Pierre Trudeau feigns to believe. Seeking to soothe the wounds Trudeau inflicted on Quebec in 1981, Mulroney has involuntarily allowed Canadian atavism to rise once more to the surface.

Quebec is at the heart of the Canadian problem. It must therefore be at the heart of the solution.

The Rules of the Game

President Lyndon Johnson campaigned in 1964 on the theme of peace, while his Republican opponent, Barry Goldwater, focused on halting the spread of communism in Indochina. Johnson scored a crushing victory. In January 1965, he began applying Goldwater's policy in Indochina. In every respect it was an American disaster, but no one challenged the legitimacy of the president.

During the election campaign of 1968, Pierre Trudeau failed to describe the real contours of his policy on bilingualism. In 1969, there appeared the Law on Official Languages. In the 1974 campaign, Trudeau ridiculed the commitment of his opponent, Conservative leader Robert Stanfield, to implement wage and price controls to suppress inflationary pressures. He scored an easy victory. By the fall of 1975, he was bringing in — wage and price controls. In 1980, he said nothing about the patriation of the Canadian constitution. And as for his solemn commitment during the referendum campaign, we now know what that was all about.

Yet no one even remotely suggested that he call a referendum or that he resign because his initiative was illegitimate.

Brian Mulroney, campaigning for the Conservative leadership in the spring of 1983, flatly turned down the idea of a free trade deal with the United States. It was a proposal endorsed by his main adversary, John Crosbie. During the 1984 federal election campaign, Mulroney said nothing about free trade and did not repudiate his earlier position. But, in the spring of 1986, he approached Ronald Reagan with the idea of opening negotiations on a free trade agreement. No one asked for a referendum.

All these politicians acted with the strictest legality. Such are the rules of the game: an elected government is an elected government. It governs the country according to its own conception of the national interest. There is always a next election. But these rules are to be accepted only if they apply equally to all. Isn't this the meaning of the legendary British fair play?

It is also possible to conclude from this brief list that no political party can be asked to describe its future strategy during an election campaign, since it has no knowledge of the problems that might surface once it is in power.

With this description of the rules of politics, we can now look at the post-Meech period.

No doubt the formal failure of the Meech Lake Accord will trigger feverish activity in Quebec and growing anxiety, tinged with resignation, in English Canada. After the verbal fireworks typical of the Quebec discourse in the preceding months, everyone will be expecting a dramatic gesture from the Quebec government. It would be unthinkable not to mark the occasion. There must be a reaction, and a rather swift one. But what?

Raising the ante? One can hear the laughter from English Canada: "We refused them a quarter and now they ask for four of them. That's a good one! Ha ha!" Raising the ante while threatening to cut federal ties? That was played out early in 1990. Taking it up again would destroy Quebec's credibility and perpetuate the unhealthy climate with which the new decade has begun, and which is slowly destroying Canadian political life.

Only one gesture is possible, and the Liberal rank and file will have understood what it is.

They will likely meet together sooner than anticipated. That day, the premier of Quebec will be able to alter the momentum of Canadian politics by addressing the people of Quebec.

The Premier's Speech

My dear fellow citizens,

Quebec has reached a turning point in its history. As you certainly know, the efforts of your government to ensure the minimum required for the development of Quebec within Confederation have failed because of the opposition of two provinces. In reality, these provinces were able to maintain their opposition to the end simply because they had support in most of the other provinces. Unfortunately, they have been able to thwart the prime minister of Canada and his government, who have long supported this project of national reconciliation. National reconciliation was the basis of the Meech Lake Accord, so poorly understood by those who preferred a simplistic and outworn concept of Canada.

Some will say we have been wasting our time. That is not my opinion, and that is not the analysis carried out by your government. First of all, the Meech Lake Accord was signed in June 1987 by the eleven heads of government in Canada, a resolution few people thought possible at the time. Unfortunately, time has undone this superb unanimity that gave us such high hopes. In this respect, I want to point out that the clause, inserted in the constitution of 1982, giving the provinces three years to ratify a new agreement, introduces an element of extreme rigidity in the procedure for amending the fundamental law of the land.

In this sense, those who repatriated the constitution locked it up tightly, despite the injustice it did Quebec. It not only reduced Quebec's jurisdiction immediately without its consent but also left Quebec open to further raids because the amending formula rendered it defenseless before a coalition of seven other provinces. This explains why Canada had to be brought back on a course more respectful of Quebec. No, we have not been wasting our time.

However, we must take note of the new situation and draw the proper conclusions. The world today moves with unbelievable speed. One only has to look at Europe, particularly at the Eastern European countries, which have decided, belatedly it is true, to adapt to the world of today. This world, which is ours as well, is one of international economic competition, accelerated technological development, and ever larger enterprises whose component parts must be ever more efficient. The state can't take the place of entrepreneurs, but it must provide the broad context that will encourage them on the road to excellence, the only one that can ensure a high level of social solidarity.

The government of Quebec, the only one exclusively concerned with the supreme interests of the province, does not currently have all the powers necessary to map out the economic future of Quebec. These powers, let me remind you, have been claimed by all the governments of Quebec, since Jean Lesage, the greatest Liberal in Quebec history, set the Quiet Revolution in motion.

The Meech Lake Accord was only the first step towards an overhaul of the Canadian system and included only the most urgent items on the agenda. Quebec's insistence on limitations to the federal government's spending power, written into the accord, shows that the present government of Quebec has never lost sight of the problem of the division of powers. Quebec also obtained the consolidation of its authority in matters of immigration, crucial for the future, as everyone knows. Unfortunately, we have been forced back to the starting point...and nothing suggests the possibility of a breakthrough for many years.

Can we afford to wait that long without any guarantee of success? If nothing is achieved by a combination of moderate demands from Quebec and a prime minister's tireless struggle for national reconciliation, isn't it illusory to expect that we will ever be in more favourable circumstances? To ask the question is to answer it. However, Quebec cannot afford to be a simple observer in the global village.

For several years, Quebec has been penalized by the fiscal and monetary policies of the federal government.

I have already indicated that there were limits to Quebec's patience. On many occasions, I have told representatives of other provinces that Quebec would have to respond should they fail to ratify the accord, which only awards the bare minimum. The conditions set out by Quebec in 1986 remained in effect, as long as there was an agreement, until June 23, 1990. There was no question of putting Quebec on stand-by after that date.

In spite of our goodwill, we of Quebec were unable to act in concert with our Canadian partners. We must therefore act quickly to seek a solution consistent with the superior interests of Quebec and the integrity of the common Canadian home. Our interests are often similar to those of other regions in Canada. We hope to preserve these links and enhance them. However, as regards the fundamental area of domestic policy — culture, communications, social affairs, and, naturally, the general framework of our domestic economic activity — the present organization of Canada is not the best suited to the goals and needs of the people of Quebec.

Conscious of my responsibilities as premier of the only French-speaking state in North America, tomorrow, in the name of the government of Quebec, I will be asking the Liberal Party convention to accept a resolution, supported by many constituencies, dealing with the creation of a new Canadian Economic Community, founded on the mutual respect of the two founding nations.

There are two fundamental points about the new Community. First, all direct and indirect taxes paid by Quebec residents and corporations will accrue to the government of Quebec, which will renounce any fiscal claims on the rest of Canada. Your government will thereby acquire the same latitude in social and economic matters that it now enjoys in education. Second, the Canadian economic entity, with all of its freedoms, will be preserved and consolidated, once there is an agreement for dividing the assets and liabilities of the government of Canada.

The maintenance of a common currency, and hence of a single central bank, is in the interest of both nations. Its management could be assigned to a board whose members would be appointed by each government in proportion to their population. As regards defense and foreign policy, which are now in flux because of upheavals in Europe, Quebec could remain associated with Canada, except for relations with the rest of the French-speaking world.

Links within the Canadian Community would still be closer than they will be within the European Economic

Community, even after 1992. The Europe of 1993 will still be lacking a common currency, foreign policy and defense.

If the resolution is accepted by the Liberal Party, it will be submitted to the National Assembly as early as next week with the conviction that it will receive widespread support. Quebec will then be ready to start negotiations with its Canadian partners as soon as possible. With goodwill on each side, the talks could proceed rapidly to minimize concern and ensure the stability of the community. Quebec undertakes to submit the results of the negotiations to the population by way of referendum.

This marks a new start for Quebec and Canada. I have no doubt that the solidarity of Quebec and the intelligence and friendship of our Canadian friends will be present on this occasion when History beckons.

My fellow citizens, good night. A *bientôt*.

The Wild Fortnight

One can be sure that few people, particularly on the right bank of the Ottawa River, expected such a quick move. It destabilized the patchwork coalition opposing any modification of the status quo. The news went round the world, with a tremendous impact on money markets. The Canadian dollar took a dive until more realistic views prevailed in money markets and business, helped on by the developing political situation.

Uncertainty breeds instability. The premier's statement came as a shock. However, expecting as much, he remained calm. He held jokers that would ensure progress on three fronts simultaneously.

All the shots fired by Canadian and Anglo-Quebec opponents were aimed at a single spot: the presumed lack of mandate. For the first few days, Canada talked of nothing else but the fall of the dollar and the absence of a mandate. In Quebec, things were different, a re-enactment of November 15, 1976. Praise was lavished on the premier. The first polls, coming out a few days after the televised statement, showed he had the support of 65 percent of the population. Protests on the absence of a mandate faded away somewhat, and old slogans from 1980 were heard again: "Canada will not negotiate" or "There is nothing to negotiate."

Someone from Bay Street or Rue St-Jacques might tell them that, although they are riding the same horse, the racetrack has changed. A pencil and a sheet of paper explains it all with a few simple figures. The federal debt is twelve times higher than that of the Quebec government. Because of its composition (more short- than long-term loans) it is very vulnerable to momentary interest rate fluctuations. A rise of one percentage point can impose on Quebec an additional yearly outlay of about $70 million, while the corresponding burden for Ottawa is in excess of *$1.5 billion.*[1] Not *noblesse* but *déficit oblige.*

Uncertainty affected the economy of Canada as well as that of Quebec. There is only one money market, and it would be surprising if, in such a situation, portfolio managers would trade Quebec and Ontario bonds for Canadian ones! Should they give in to panic, they would choose the American dollar. Canadian bonds would feel the blow. The Bank of Canada would have its hands full defending the Canadian dollar, by raising interest rates to arrest the flight of capital...

The government of Quebec wouldn't be in such a bad situation. If need be, it could count on the Caisse de dépôt et placement. But the whole point of "Operation Instability" lies elsewhere. The extra costs amount to a net loss for Ottawa. Things are very different with Quebec, which can expect a net gain of *at least* $1 billion a year by bringing its marbles home from Ottawa. This fact will help to cushion a few weeks of rocky weather and face the storm unleashed by stock exchanges and money markets. In addition, Quebec manufacturers find the Canadian dollar to be overvalued. So this is not David facing Goliath, or Lithuania against the Soviet Union.

Industrial and financial circles in Canada would soon voice the opinion that the marriage of the Maple Leaf with the Fleur-de-Lis isn't worth this whirlwind (particularly when most economic indicators are already sliding), and that the two governments might do well to sit down at the same table. They will say that this premier of Quebec is preferable to the leader of the Parti Québécois. "The devil we know is better than the one we don't."

And then the National Assembly had just passed with a very big majority the resolution proposing a New Canadian Community. Only anglophone members voted against it. Others swallowed hard...since the premier made the whole issue a matter of confidence. A large number of Canadians told themselves how embarrassing it was to go against such a clear expression of the popular will, particularly as Canada had no alternative to offer.

Finally, the premier's proposal didn't seem so extravagant after all. He started circulating a little chart comparing his New Canadian Community (NCC) with the advancement of the European Economic Community at the beginning of 1991. One saw that, with respect to integration and cooperation, that the NCC was way ahead of the EEC. The argument about going against the current of history was in trouble.

The Canadian government had lost its bearings. Contradictory signals were coming from the media and from all parts of the country. To negotiate or not to negotiate? Conservatives from Quebec were pressing the prime minister to opt for the first solution, but without making a fuss. It was a very delicate situation. How could a Canadian prime minister from Quebec possibly negotiate in Canada's name the "secession" of his home province? A tricky proposition. And shouldn't there be one last battle to prevent the breakup of the country? It was obvious, however, that he couldn't do anything without the support of the Quebec caucus, which sided more or less with Quebec.

Comparison of the New Canadian Community and the European Economic Community
January 1, 1991

	NCC	EEC
Free movement of persons	Yes	Minimal customs controls for nationals Customs controls for foreigners
Free movement of internal capital	Yes	Beginning July 1, 1990
Free movement of workers	Yes with exceptions	More or less for nationals None for foreign workers
Immigration policy	Two	Twelve
Citizenship	One, accessible	Twelve, difficult
Monetary policy	One	Quite a few, although subject to constraints
Fiscal policy	Two with constraints	Twelve
Income gap between rich and poor areas	1.5 to 1.0	5 to 1
Defense policy	Two armies one common policy	Twelve armies several policies
Foreign policy	Important common thread	Several common points Many discordant policies
Charter of minority language rights	Yes	No

Meanwhile, the Canadian finance minister was seeing red. Every attempt to deal with the deficit, causing the ruling party's popularity to sink, would come to nothing if this basic problem was not resolved very soon. But few of his cabinet colleagues were eager to get their feet wet, fearing the political consequences of being soft on Canada. No one wanted to be called the Canadian Chamberlain.*

The premier of Quebec went around repeating that his plan safeguarded the essential point, the integrity of economic links with Canada, and that the new political arrangement did not put in doubt the friendship of Quebecers for Canadians. He had even committed himself to enshrining the rights of Quebec anglophones in a charter of minority rights to be annexed to the founding treaty of the New Canadian Community. But to bring the period of instability to an end, it was urgent to agree on a general draft. Accountants would have plenty of time later to assess the value of railway lines, highways, and buildings belonging to the federal government, and to split in a fair way the federal public debt.

No doubt English Canada would have accepted the proposition in the end. The positive aspects of Quebec's gesture were beginning to emerge: no more constitutional quarrels or language conflicts. Some people saw the prospect of a stronger Canadian government, while political parties calculated their own chances in the new Canada. Others claimed that the refusal to take Quebec's extended hand risked a real breakup of this two-headed country.

The idea of holding a referendum at the *end* rather than at the beginning of the whole process seemed to be the winning one. It had two objectives: to place the burden of instability on the country as a whole and to force the Canadian government to play its hand *before* an electoral consultation in Quebec. How can one ask the population to give its opinion of some initiative whose institutional ramifications are largely unknown?

---

* Neville Chamberlain was the British Prime Minister who, in 1938, had taken a very conciliatory attitude towards Adolf Hitler at the Munich Conference, which brought about the cession of part of Czechoslovakia to Germany.

No one was thinking about the new leader of the Opposition in the House of Commons and his confederates in the wings.

Finesse Royal

There was nothing surprising in his intervention. The Liberal Party of Canada had long believed itself the legitimate depository of power: it had ruled the country almost without interruption from 1921 to 1984. But without Quebec, it had little chance of regaining its former position. It had to strike a powerful blow. Since it had lost power in 1984, the party still had a master card, which it had used on two occasions. It would serve once again.

It was with a great pomp that the new leader of the Liberal Party announced that he would never allow the prime minister to destroy the country, claiming that neither Canada nor Quebec had any mandate for this sinister job, and promised he would use the Senate's veto if necessary to block any legislation authorizing Canada-Quebec negotiations. The new leader's occasional "godfather" applauded openly, hoping his prestige would tip the scales. Apparently, the people of Quebec would never be free of him. The duo put forward a very simple solution to end the deadlock, a referendum in Quebec asking voters "Are you in favour of Quebec independence?"

A short digression is in order at this point.

The Canadian Senate has a poor media image in Quebec. In fact, it is an intriguing problem for any democrat. If the criterion of democracy is the rule of law, in so far as laws are voted democratically, then the Senate can legitimately make use of the powers conferred under the constitution, including the refusal to ratify laws passed by the House of Commons. Democracy is sometimes incongruous, but the Senate and its powers survived in the constitution of 1982, adopted by the House of Commons by a wide majority.

The example shows that accepting the rules of the

game does not always come easy. The paradox becomes more complicated when the Senate supports what we all consider the foundation of democracy, the right of citizens to pass judgement on particularly important pieces of legislation. This was the case when the Senate, at the request of John Turner, forced the Conservative government to go before the voters with the Free Trade Agreement before ratifying it. Unfortunately, few commentators seem to have understood that, if one happened to believe in democracy, it was possible to support both John Turner's decision *and* the Free Trade Agreement. End of digression.

But one can always be outsmarted. The Liberal opposition's decision to block the beginning of a dialogue between Quebec and Ottawa was the straw that broke the camel's back in Quebec; it also drew the reprobation of English Canada, which thought it was an incendiary gesture. The premier of Quebec saw an opening allowing him to use his fourth joker — and to alter once again the dynamics of the situation to his advantage.

The quick succession of events took everyone by surprise. The ball started rolling when the Conservative minister from Lac St-Jean, head of the Quebec wing of the caucus, rose in the House of Commons to read in French a statement prepared by the government at a special all-night meeting. It was also read in English by the deputy prime minister, who still enjoyed modest credibility in English Canada. The statement announced a three-point plan to end the stalemate.

First of all, a draft treaty would immediately be signed with Quebec to guarantee, whatever happened, the maintenance of the Canadian economic union and of the Canadian currency. The plumbing was safe.

Secondly, a referendum would be held on the same day in Quebec and in English Canada, at the earliest possible moment. The question would be identical, except for two words. In Quebec, responsibility for the referendum would fall on the provincial government, which, after consultation, had agreed to the wording of the question:

> The Government of Quebec wishes to repatriate all taxes paid by Quebecers to the Canadian Government and exempt Quebec from Canadian laws, while preserving the Canadian common market and the Canadian currency, the foundations of the New Canadian Community. Are you ready to give the Government of Quebec a mandate to negotiate these points speedily and in good faith with the Government of Canada?

In the question addressed to English Canada, where the referendum was to be held under federal authority, the words Quebec and Canada were interchanged in the last sentence.

The law making the referendum possible would be introduced as quickly as possible in Parliament.

The move did not necessarily thwart possible obstruction by the Senate. Hence, the third paragraph in the statement, which reasserted the government's intention to obtain amicably or otherwise the Senate's assent to the referendum bill. End of statement.

The opposition was obviously stunned, particularly the Liberals. Their threat of obstruction had boomeranged. Some New Democrats, nimble with figures, were already assessing their chances of becoming the official Opposition in the new Canada.

A great many people were surprised at the absence of the prime minister on this historic day. They did not have to wait long for an answer. A terse communiqué from the Prime Minister's Office, that very evening, disclosed that he had resigned his political functions. The failure of the Canada he had known and loved was also his own, and he had drawn the proper conclusions.

Stockbrokers and money traders worked as hard that day as they had on preceding ones, but the atmosphere was certainly more relaxed. Investors were bargain-hunting, and there was no lack of opportunities. People had lost their heads for a while, but in the end the New Canadian Community was still the land of the future, whatever its name, wasn't it?

The United States and France quickly dispatched telegrams of congratulation to the deputy prime minister, who was acting as caretaker until the Conservative Party chose a temporary successor for the former prime minister.

The premier of Quebec knew that evening that he had won the game of a lifetime. The rest was just a series of formalities.

The Great Clarification

Political reporters managed to piece together the events leading to this dramatic dénouement. The reconstituted story was as follows.

Anger was running high in the Quebec Conservative caucus, ever since the Liberal leader of the opposition had put his cards on the table. Many MPs, remembering the days of May 1980 and November 1981, felt it was now or never.

A few of them worked out a strategy supported by a majority in the caucus. The situation required a common front, complete solidarity. From the very beginning of the crisis, ministers had been in constant contact with Quebec. The background of the historic statement was coming into view. The idea of a national referendum had taken most people by surprise. Many thought it was a trap, but finally understood that it was the logical outcome of the course chosen by Quebec.

The policy of the outstretched hand to English Canada required some mechanism allowing English-Canadian groups, who were eager to reciprocate but unwilling to go public about their feelings, to express their views. It was a checkered coalition, if ever there was one. It included friends of Quebec, people who were fed up with bilingualism (half the population), and the diehards who wanted Quebec out. It comprised a large number of people. The idea of the referendum also signaled that a page had been turned and that the time had come to think of the future. In this context, common sense was on the Yes side.

English Canada's Yes would not necessarily be enthusiastic. However, that English-Canadians were getting a chance to decide on a historic change directly concerning them gave the Yes campaign an important psychological advantage, which helped Quebec's cause. Moreover, public opinion polls could be expected to create a strong movement in English Canada in favour of the Yes side, particularly because of its very strong and early lead in Quebec.

Post-referendum negotiations would therefore proceed much more smoothly, with troublemakers out of the way.

But how could this simple and elegant solution be imposed on the Canadian government? The minister from Lac St-Jean was given the mission, requiring all the diplomacy of which he was capable. He also had plenty of ammunition and had the support of almost all of the other ministers from Quebec, who had put aside their disagreements for the occasion.

He could also count on the support of the Bloc Québécois, which gathered behind the charismatic figure of a former ambassador to France quite a few ex-Conservatives, and even some ex-Liberals.*

The message was a simple one. The government could accept the three conditions (to be made public the next day), continue in power after the referendum, and enter into negotiations with Quebec. It would thus become the first government of the new Canada and earn the public's grati-

*This sentence has been added to the English edition.

tude for having skilfully steered the ship through the storm and avoided the worst. Or it could reject the three conditions, in which case it forfeited the support of the Quebec caucus. Ministers from English Canada winced, being aware of the latest poll results. An election at this moment would be disastrous for the country, and would certainly bring about the destruction of their party in English Canada.

The prime minister violently objected to the proposal of his Quebec minister. But he was alone. The alternative he proposed was a constitutional conference of eleven heads of government, which seemed ridiculous in the context. Someone made the remark that this possibility had been closed since June 23, 1990.

All members of the government were aware of the choice before them: a showdown with Quebec, whose outcome and consequences no one could predict, or a new kind of political community. Canadians were basically reasonable people who wanted only one thing: get this Quebec business over with once and for all. But now the choice was between the prime minister and a more serene future. Politics is not an easy game. Many of them were holding back tears as the prime minister shook their hands one last time before disappearing into the night.

End of the reconstitution.

Announcement of the national referendum took everyone by surprise. The Liberal opposition was completely nonplussed when the government took its suggestion literally, deciding to consult the population. It had little credibility in Quebec, home of its leader. It could hardly campaign for the No west of Quebec without risking serious accusations. Wasn't this the party that had ruthlessly tried to build an impossible Canada, which had misled English Canada about the true feelings of Quebec? And it continued to fan the flames?

Voters were eager to get it over with. A single cry emerged from English Canada: *Referendum now!* Members of the Senate made themselves scarce. The referendum bill was given three readings in quick succession in the House of Commons; just enough senators turned up for speedy approval by the Senate.

A number of developments during the referendum campaign came as no surprise to attentive observers of the Canadian scene. First, few groups in English Canada openly supported the No, except in the Maritime provinces, whose geographic situation was now thought very unfavourable. The Maritimes insisted on comparing themselves with the Pakistan of old, while others suggested that Alaska might be more appropriate. French minorities across Canada were in mourning, in spite of various proposals for a charter of minority language rights, and even though a few had come to the conclusion that the future, with or without Quebec, was not bright. The anglophone minority in Quebec waged a lonely campaign for the No. It was a far cry from the heady days of 1980.

Everyone else had reasons for voting Yes. Ontario was eager to preserve close economic ties with Quebec. The western provinces saw Quebec's departure as an opportunity to play an expanded role in the new Canadian federation, whose centre of gravity would necessarily be shifting westward. The Reform Party, the rising star of Canadian politics, was campaigning enthusiastically for the Yes.

Finally, the campaign allowed national parties, who were feeling their way carefully (except for the Reform Party) in the new political configuration, a kind of dress rehearsal.

Canadian Liberals finally grasped what a disastrous choice they had made on June 23, 1990, when the leadership was taken over by a Quebecer who had once been highly popular in English Canada. Events had moved incredibly fast. The new leader was now resigned to the inevitable. He was the wrong man at the wrong place at the wrong time. The party had gone downhill and a new "salesman" was necessary. The choice quickly focused on a woman who had made a good impression during the long leadership campaign in the first half of 1990.

The referendum campaign constituted a period of reflection on the future of the new Canada. Topics of discussion were not lacking: should certain provinces be merged for better use of available human resources? Was a new constitution necessary? The west was highly impatient over the Senate, which would certainly be reformed. On the other hand, the possibility of joining the United States was hardly mentioned. The omission confirmed the views of a renowned American sociologist who concluded, at the end of the eighties, that Canada and the United States were like two trains that, after traveling along parallel lines for quite a long distance, found themselves after two hundred years as far from each other as ever.[2]

Many observers thought the campaign in English Canada was the more interesting, the Quebec one becoming repetitive for lack of serious opposition.

The outcome of the double vote soon became self-evident.

The premier of Quebec thus enjoyed a strategic success worthy of George Patton, one of the celebrated generals of this century. Quick to spot openings and take advantage of them, Patton could not resist being sarcastic about his rival, General Montgomery, whose wait-and-see tactics proved to be extremely costly for the Anglo-American Allies in 1944 and 1945. The premier, with the support of public opinion, had masterfully played the card of instability. He had never been a peddler of dreams. He was content to be the man of common sense.

His happiness was marred only by one vexing little cloud. Some friendships had been lost, probably forever. But hadn't politics always been his first love?

D-Day

The treaty defining the legal framework and the institutions of the New Canadian Community was negotiated quickly and in good faith. Many passages were borrowed from the Canada–U.S. Free Trade Agreement and from the regulations of the European Economic Community. More contentious questions, such as sharing the assets of Crown corporations, were to be submitted to the newly created Court of the Community.

On D-Day, all assets of the federal government in Quebec became the property of the Quebec government, which renounced all property claims on the rest of Canada. Quebec's estimated share of the federal public debt was added to its own. All federal civil servants working in Quebec kept the same offices and the same bosses. Quebecers working for the federal government in Ottawa were relocated for the most part to Hull in comparable jobs. A few years would be needed to rationalize all this.

All federally chartered companies obtained charters from Quebec.

Obviously, there would be another anglophone exodus from Montreal, which would be partly offset this time by an influx of former federal civil servants and francophones from other parts of Canada who were finally deciding to live as members of a majority.

Some companies were hesitant about investing in Quebec. However, the government planned to make use of its greater budgetary leeway to support basic research, the restructuring of Quebec firms, and their participation in international trade. The government also planned to fully use for marketing purposes Quebec's social and cultural distinctiveness. Furthermore, many mandarins, who had made the jump from Ottawa to Quebec, were eager to get down to work.

Many analysts were beginning to take bets on the chances of the former province and of the New Canadian Community. In the year 2000, would they be speaking about the economic miracle of Quebec, or of its economic demise?

The answer to this question rested with about seven million people. There could be no scapegoats now.

This will be another story altogether. We know for sure that it will have its share of surprises.

Epilogue

Two nations, who do not dislike each other (too much), are about to set their public affairs in order and draw the line on half a century of conflicts and recriminations. They will exchange a difficult and costly cohabitation for a cooperative relationship, which has every chance of being simple and fruitful. What France and Germany have achieved, in spite of the very painful events of the past — would be that out of reach for Quebec and Canada?

There are some who believe that the balkanization of Canada, followed by annexion to the United States, will be inevitable after Quebec's political exit. In other words, Quebec has been simultaneously the most discordant unit of Confederation and its cement! This is a paradox for students of philosophy. We tend to forget that people in the rest of Canada will recover *their* homeland and that their desire for independence is just as keen as Quebec's.

These two nations might have understood each other if merchants of illusion had not been so long in power. With a great deal of arrogance, they proposed unattainable goals. They had self-confidence and believed they were in tune with the thrust of History, when in fact they perched on one of the accidental peaks of the century. History is following its course, and these utopians from another age will disappear from its rearview mirror.

The failure of the Meech Lake Accord, the irrationality of Canadian federalism and its attending costs, will inspire Quebec to cut the Gordian knot. Who knows if the project for a new Canadian community will not become a model for European countries trying to come to grips with the inextricable problem of nationalities?

Time will pass and, some day, people will wonder about these Byzantine discussions on the pertinence of a solution wholly in line with contemporary developments.

And others will come to join us, participating with us in the growth of Quebec, this French land in America.

Endnotes

Chapter 1

1. See particularly Dale C. Thomson, *Jean Lesage and the Quiet Revolution,* Macmillan of Canada, Toronto, 1984.

2. In 1960, the Liberal Party received 51 percent of the vote and the Union Nationale 47 percent. Non-francophones constituted 19 percent of the population and had largely voted Liberal.

3. *Report of the Royal Commission on Bilingualism and Biculturalism,* Volume III, "The Work World," The Queen's Printer for Canada, Ottawa, 1969.

4. Pierre Elliott Trudeau, "Quebec and the Constitutional Problem," in *Federalism and the French Canadians,* Macmillan, Toronto, 1980, p. 5.

5. *Report of the Royal Commission of Inquiry on Constitutional Problems,* Province of Quebec, 1956, p. 94.

6. Maurice Lamontagne, *Le fédéralisme canadien,* Les Presses de l'Université Laval, Quebec, 1954.

7. Michel Vastel, *Trudeau le Québécois,* L'Homme, Montreal, 1989, p. 124.

Chapter 2

1. Trudeau's constitutional vision was expressed, in 1965, in an important essay, "Québec and the Constitutional Problem," which was published two years later. *Op. cit.*

2. Ibid, p. 49-50.

3. Christina McCall-Newman has notably written *Grits, An Intimate Portrait of the Liberal Party,* Macmillan, Toronto, 1982.

4. René Lévesque, *Memoirs,* McClelland & Stewart, Toronto, 1986.

5. Pierre Elliott Trudeau, *op. cit.*, p. 24.

6. Georges Mathews, *Le choc démographique,* Boréal Express, Montreal, 1984.

7. Richard Joy, *Languages in Conflict,* McClelland & Stewart, Toronto, 1972.

8. Richard Gwyn, *The Northern Magus,* PaperJacks, Markham, 1981, pp. 222-230.

9. Dale C. Thomson, *op. cit.*, p. 321.

10. Jean-Louis Roy, *Le choix d'un pays: Le débat constitutionnel Québec-Canada, 1960–1976*, Leméac, Montreal, 1978.

11. Peter Brimelow, *The Patriot Game, Canada and the Canadian Question Revisited*, Hoover Institution Press, Stanford, 1986, p. 5.

12. Robert Bourbeau, *Canada — A Linguistic Profile*, Statistics Canada, Reference No. 98-131, December 1989.

13. Georges Mathews, *op. cit.*

14. Frank Howard, "The Official Languages and Federal Public Servants," in *Language and Society*, Special Report, Summer 1989, p. R-23.

15. Commissioner of Official Languages, *Annual Report 1987*, Ottawa, p. 44.

16. Ibid., p. 222.

17. Ibid., p. 220.

18. Richard Gwyn, *op. cit.*, p. 248.

19. Neil Morrison, "Bilingualism and Biculturalism," in *Language and Society*, Special Report, Summer 1989, p. R-8.

20. Commissioner of Official Languages, *Annual Report*, Ottawa, various years.

21. Yves Lusignan, "After Official Bilingualism," in *Language and Society*, Fall 1989, p. 22.

See also, concerning the teaching of French in English Canada: Peat, Marwick and Partners, *Evaluation of the Official Languages in Education Program*, Report to the Secretary of State (Ottawa), May 1987.

Chapter 3

1. See Richard Gwyn, *op. cit.*, and Michel Vastel, *op. cit.*

2. The annual reports of the Commissioner of Official Languages trace these judicial sagas.

3. This information comes from the documentary film of Donald Brittain, *The Champions III, The Final Battle*, National Film Board, 1986.

Chapter 4

1. See Claude Morin, *Le pouvoir québécois en négociation*, Boréal Express, Montreal, 1972.

2. Department of Finance Canada, *Annual Reference Tables*, June 1989.

3. Statistics Canada, Catalogue 13-213S, *Provincial Economic Accounts 1961–1986*, June 1988, and Ministère des Finances du Québec, *Budget*, different years.

4. Department of Finance Canada, *The Budget*, February 20, 1990.

5. Government of Canada, *Federal-Provincial Programs and Activities, A Descriptive Inventory, 1988–1989*, Ottawa, June 1989.

6. Department of Finance, Canada, *Equalization Payments*, March 1987.

7. See Jean-Louis Roy, *op. cit.*, and Richard Gwyn, *op. cit.*

8. Claude Morin, *op. cit.*

9. Pierre Elliott Trudeau, *op. cit.*, pp. 40-41.

10. Pierre Elliott Trudeau, "The Practice and Theory of Federalism," *op. cit.*, p. 136.

11. See Jacques Monet, *The Last Cannon Shot*, University of Toronto Press, Toronto, 1969. Unfortunately, the author does not discuss public administration during this period.

12. Seymour Martin Lipset, *Continental Divide: The Values and Institutions of the United States and Canada*, Routledge, New York, 1990, Chapter 11.

Chapter 5

1. Richard Gwyn, *op. cit.*, pp. 331 and 332.

2. Claude Morin, *Lendemains piégés, Du référendum à la nuit des longs couteaux*, Boréal, Montreal, 1988, p. 14.

3. Robert Sheppard and Michael Valpy, *The National Deal: The Fight for a Canadian Constitution*, Fleet Books, Toronto, 1982, p. 5.

4. Ibid, pp. 76 and 77.

5. Ibid, p. 300

6. Pierre Elliott Trudeau, "Quebec and the Constitutional Problem," *op. cit.*, p. 39.

7. Donald Johnston, ed., *With a Bang, Not a Whimper: Pierre Trudeau Speaks Out*, Stoddart, Toronto, 1988.

8. See the interesting exchange of letters between René Lévesque and Pierre Trudeau on this question, in Claude Morin, *op. cit.*, pp. 354 to 359.

9. Jean Chrétien, "Bringing the Constitution Home," in *Towards a Just Society: The Trudeau Years*, Thomas S. Axworthy and Pierre Elliott Trudeau, eds., Viking, Markham, 1990.

10. Pierre Bourgault, *Moi, je m'en souviens*, Stanké, Montreal, 1989.

11. Constitutional Commission of the Liberal Party of Quebec, *A New Canadian Federation*, January 1980.

Chapter 6

1. See in particular Jeffrey Simpson, "His feelings then, his remarks now," *The Globe and Mail*, January 4, 1990.

2. See the account of Michel Vastel in *Le Devoir*, June 4, 1987. This article and many others have been gathered in "Un Dossier du Devoir," *Le Québec et le lac Meech*, Guérin Littérature, Montreal, 1987.

3. In a long article published simultaneously in *La Presse* and *The Toronto Star*, May 27, 1987.

4. "Un Dossier du Devoir," *op. cit.*, p. 57.

5. Donald Johnston, *op. cit.* p. 148.

6. The detailed comments of Pierre Trudeau on the Meech Lake Accord have been presented in a series of texts gathered by Donald Johnston, *op. cit.* The French version of these texts was not published until a year later by HMH.

7. Ibid, p. 97.

8. Calculations based on results published in newspapers of November 22, 1988.

9. Donald Johnston, *op. cit.*, p. 157.

Chapter 7

1. See preface by Paul-André Linteau in *Histoire Générale du Canada* (French edition edited by Paul-André Linteau), Boréal, Montreal, 1988.

2. Robert Bourbeau, *op. cit.*, p. 31.

3. Gilles Pronovost, *Les comportements des Québécois en matière d'activités culturelles de loisir en 1989*, Éditeur officiel du Québec, June 1990.

4. William Tetley, *Les droits linguistiques du point de vue d'un anglophone*, conference given at ACFAS congress, Montreal, May 17, 1989, p. 17.

5. François Vaillancourt and Josée Carpentier, *Le contrôle de l'économie du Québec: la place des francophones en 1987 et son évolution depuis 1961*, Office de la langue française, July 1989.

6. These demolinguistic projections were realized in 1989 by Jacques Ledent, professor at INRS-Urbanisation.

7. Pierre Drouilly published an interesting article on this topic in *Le Devoir*, a few days after the election.

See also:

Marcel Côté, "Les conséquences économiques de l'insularité linguistique du Québec," in *L'Actualité économique*, September 1988.

Liberté, "Strangers in Paradise/Étranglés au Québec.," June 1989.

Chapter 8

1. This idea was expressed in: Georges Mathews, "Le nouvel ordre européen," *Le Devoir*, December 2, 1989.

2. David Buchan and Tim Dickson, "Tying Germany to a United Europe," *Financial Times*, March 27, 1990.

3. Philippe Moreau-Defarges, "L'Acte unique européen," in *L'état du monde 1988–1989*, La Découverte, Paris, 1988, p. 480.

4. Françoise Lazare, "Trois étapes pour faire l'union économique et monétaire européenne," *Le Monde*, April 18, 1989.

At the end of spring 1990, no book has yet appeared on the revolution of 1989 and its ramifications. Various annuals (*Ramses*, published by l'Institut français des relations internationales, and *L'état du monde*) provide useful information but have clearly been outstripped by events. Those interested in these questions should regularly consult *Sélection hebdomadaire du Monde* and *The Economist* of London, the most complete and analytical of the weeklies.

Chapter 9

1. *La Presse*, December 27, 1989. Poll taken by Sorécom.

2. Jean-Paul Gagné, "Le fédéralisme n'est plus rentable" (interview with Jacques Parizeau), *Les Affaires*, March 10–16, 1990.

3. Statistics Canada, Catalogue 13-213S, *op. cit.*

4. Jean-Paul Gagné, *op. cit.*

5. C. Bloskie, "An Overview of Different Measures of Government Deficits and Debt," in Statistics Canada, *Canadian Economic Observer*, November 1989, pp. 3.1–3.20.

6. Department of Finance Canada, *The Budget*, February 20, 1990, p. 121.

7. Data derived from the following sources: Bureau de la statistique du Québec, *La situation économique au Québec, édition 1988*, Québec, 1988; Yves Rabeau, *Impact du libre-échange sur le marché du travail*, Université de Montréal, February 1989.

8. *The Financial Times* and *The Economist*, both of London, are closely monitoring the debates.

Chapter 10

1. Data on debt and on annual financing needs are found in the budgets of the two governments.

2. Seymour Martin Lipset, *op. cit.*, p. 212.

DRUMBEAT

Anger and Renewal in Indian Country

EDITED BY BOYCE RICHARDSON

A startling collection of essays from Canada's foremost Native leaders, with an introduction from Georges Erasmus. This book constitutes an essential primer for readers interested in a balanced view of the history of Canada's relations with its indigenous peoples.

$14.95, paper ISBN 0-929091-18-3

CLOSING THE DOORS:

The Failure of Refugee Protection in Canada

DAVID MATAS WITH ILANA SIMON

A passionate yet concise documentation of the failure of Canada's refugee protection legislation, written by one of the country's foremost immigration lawyers. Closing The Doors traces the roots of our current stance towards refugee protection and argues against the long term damage of this policy. This book is elemental in any understanding of the refugee question.

$24.95, cloth ISBN 0-920197-81-7